Warning! Revelation is about to be fulfilled

Larry Wilson

Copyright © 1997

Wake Up America Seminars, Inc.
P.O. Box 273, Bellbrook, Ohio 45305
(513) 848-3322

First printing, March 1988
Second printing, June 1990
Third printing, January 1991
Fourth printing, November 1992
Fifth printing, June 1994
Sixth printing, June 1997

Printed by

Teach Services
Donivan Road
Route 1, Box 182
Brushton, New York 12916-9738

Acknowledgments

This book is dedicated to those who are longing for the return of our Savior, our Lord and our Friend, Jesus Christ.

This printing of *Warning! Revelation is about to be fulfilled* has been made possible through the generosity of donors who wish to remain anonymous. Even though tens of thousands of readers will never know the identity of their benefactors – God knows what has been done in secret, and He will reward accordingly.

Special appreciation is also due Marty, Shelley, Gail, Sam and Ronni for their help on this edition. Even more, I am forever indebted to a dedicated staff (both paid and unpaid), generous volunteers and a rapidly growing number of wonderful people world-wide who understand this message and faithfully support this unique ministry.

Wake Up America Seminars, Inc. is a non-profit, educational organization. WUAS is not affiliated, endorsed nor sponsored by any religious organization. Our mission is to proclaim salvation and herald the imminent return of our Lord, Jesus Christ, through whatever means possible.

Warning! Revelation is about to be fulfilled

Table of Contents

Chapter 1
The Rendezvous

Revelation predicts a number of incredible events that will soon occur. These events will not happen in random order nor will they be freak manifestations of violent weather. The coming events predicted in Revelation are carefully designed and executed by the Creator of Heaven and Earth. The following is a chronological list of these events:

1. Four earthquakes will violently shake the whole Earth during a time span of about 1,335 days. (Revelation 8:5; 11:13; 11:19; 16:18; Daniel 12:11,12) These earthquakes have had no equal in recorded history. The Richter scale will not be able to measure the magnitude of these "global earthquakes." These earthquakes will increase in intensity as they occur. The first earthquake will mark the beginning of the "end-time," the commencement of the Great Tribulation. The fourth and final earthquake will be so violent that it will move *all* the mountains and islands from their places. (Revelation 16:20; 6:14) One aspect that makes this prophecy particularly interesting is that until the early 1990's, many geologists claimed a global earthquake was impossible.

2. Shortly (perhaps 30 days) after the first global earthquake, showers of white-hot hailstones will pummel this planet.

Meteoric firestorms will ignite great fires all over the world. Billions of acres of rain forests, food crops and vegetation will be destroyed in a few days. In addition, hundreds of millions of people will either perish, be left homeless or suffer greatly from severe burns resulting from this "rain of terror." (Revelation 8:7)

3. Following the meteoric showers of burning hail, Earth will experience two horrific asteroid impacts – the first will hit an ocean; the second will strike a continent. (Revelation 8:8-11) The ocean impact will create a series of tidal waves that will destroy many large coastal cities. People of all nations will be frightened and distressed from the consequence of this impact. (Luke 21:25) The oceans will turn violent and man will be powerless. Seaports and coastal cities will completely disappear. The second asteroid impact will affect one of Earth's continents and cause extensive death by contaminating the water supply. Ground waves from the impact will fracture septic lines and toxic waste sites allowing deadly bacteria to enter underground aquifers. The seismic havoc radiating from the impact site will destroy the geological integrity of "safe" land fills. The leakage of lethal chemicals and radioactive waste into underground streams will contaminate drinking water for thousands of square miles. Revelation predicts that many people will die from drinking poisonous water.

4. The asteroid impacts will cause the tectonic plates deep within the Earth to shift. These shifts will trigger numerous volcanic eruptions which will destroy large cities (and many

people). (Revelation 8:12) The jet stream will convey ash, soot and debris around the world in clouds of dense darkness for months on end. The absence of direct sunlight over the middle third of the Earth will prevent remaining crops from reaching maturity. In areas fortunate enough to miss the enormous firestorms described above, the darkness caused by volcanic debris will affect food harvests, even though crops may be located hundreds, even thousands of miles away from the volcanos. In short, this development will insure global famine.

5. Several months (possibly 24?) after the volcano eruptions, the devil himself will physically appear on Earth and claim to be Almighty God. (Revelation 9:1-11; 2 Thessalonians 2:1-12; Revelation 13:11-18) Deceptively cloaked in brilliant glory and charming benevolence, the devil will claim that (1) he is God, and (2) that he has come to establish a thousand years of peace on Earth. Because of his splendor and the marvelous miracles he will perform – even calling fire down from heaven to prove his assumed divinity – billions (that is billions) of people will believe his lies and obey him with a zeal and devotion that will be astounding. The devil himself, in the form of a glorious God-man, is the Antichrist of Revelation.

6. Eventually, the devil (the Antichrist) will convince his followers to destroy anyone who refuses to recognize him as God. There will be a great war, extended suffering, persecution and eventually, martyrdom for all who refuse to submit to the devil's demands. The devil will gain control of

the religious and political powers of Earth and establish a world government that will issue a command requiring all inhabitants of Earth to receive a mark on their right hand or on their foreheads. The mark will either be a tatoo showing the number "666" on the right hand, or if the person is an official in Satan's government, the mark of the beast will be a tatoo of the devil's name worn on the forehead. (Revelation 13:11-18) The devil and his forces will ultimately gain complete dominion of Earth for a short period.

World's Infrastructure Destroyed

According to the time-periods identified in the book of Revelation, the first four catastrophic events could be fulfilled during a very short period of time, perhaps 30 to 60 days. The magnitude, extent and rapidity of these horrible events will cause every person alive to have three questions. First, how can the human race survive? Great terror and overwhelming bewilderment will naturally fill the hearts of the people who survive these incredible catastrophes. Think about the consequences of such global destruction. Every infrastructure will be demolished. Communication, travel, commerce, education, agriculture, healthcare and governmental assistance will be almost nonexistent. The second question everyone will ask is what great calamity is coming next? The rapid-fire sequence of the first four events suggests that more terror is coming. Anticipation and anxiety will produce many dysfunctional people. Very few people are mentally or spiritually prepared to cope with the hardships that are forthcoming and physical preparation is practically useless. God plans to inflict a mortal blow to Earth. His purpose is to awaken Earth's inhabitants to their true spiritual condition and reveal the prerequisites of His coming kingdom. Through this sequence of coming events God will separate the multitudes of Earth into two categories: The people who love Him and those who do not. The third question that will rise during this time will be the authority and reach of God's law. The subject of God's wrath will come to the forefront of religious and nonreligious minds. These three questions and man's attempt to answer them within the context of God's cataclysmic manifestations will produce the human response that Revelation predicts.

Man's Response to God's Judgments

The following is a brief statement about man's response to the first of God's judgments:

1. A worldwide religious coalition will quickly form in response to the first four horrific events. Revelation calls this coalition "Babylon" because in many ways, its behavior will parallel ancient Babylon. (Ancient Babylonian kings were noted for directly opposing the God of Heaven.) The coalition will include leaders from all religions of the world. Almost overnight, this coalition will spearhead a global religious revolution that springs from terror. The coalition's message will be simple: "God is angry with the sinful ways of man. We must repent and honor God or He will soon destroy the rest of the world." Obviously, survivors will be seeking answers and explanations from their clergy who will boldly step forward to "guide their sheep" through this

most distressing hour. But, the clergy's bravado will prove to be little more than foolish vanity. The formation of the coalition and the solutions it pursues will prove that most clergy do not understand God's Word, intentions or plans. (Remember how God embarrassed Nebuchadnezzar's wise men? See Daniel 2.) If the clergy understood God's plans, they would not join or support the apostate and blasphemous coalition that will form. Leaders of the coalition will claim to have answers that satisfy God, but their actions will prove to be contrary, even defiant to God's will. Their ignorance and vanity will become obvious to survivors as the tribulation continues. Many church-going people will become disoriented and keenly disappointed with the "experts."

Consider the compelling forces that propel this worldwide religious coalition into existence. Common (that is, community) suffering is a powerful instrument that brings diverse groups of people together. Sociologists have long observed the "community effect" that occurs when a diverse group of people experience a common disaster. For example, Hurricane Andrew nearly wiped Homestead, Florida off the map in August 1992. The overwhelming destruction of Homestead created a new "Homestead," a new community of friendship and caring. People lived next door to each other for years without even knowing their neighbor's name, but the hurricane changed everything. Suddenly, everyone was "in the same boat together." Talk about "fellow-ship!" In just one night, neighbors became acquainted. They needed, trusted and depended upon each other to survive – the typical human response to common suffering.

Common suffering also produces the "community effect" on a national scale. Before the War Between the States in the 1860's, citizens referred to the United States in the plural. For example they would say, "The United States *are* governed by a Congress of Representatives." After the Civil War, Americans referred to the United States in the singular. "The United States *is* governed by a Congress of Representatives." The suffering caused by the Civil War transformed many states into one nation.

Because the events described earlier are global in nature, they will affect *all* of Earth's inhabitants. People will suffer *together* in one way or another from a common cause. According to Revelation 6:8, 25% of Earth's population will perish during these coming events. Earth's present population is approximately six billion, so this means 1.5 billion people will perish worldwide. Since the flood in Noah's day, this planet has not seen such comprehensive destruction. Global devastations will bring all nations together in common suffering. Suddenly, the infighting and bickering of nations will stop. Everyone will suddenly realize that man is accountable to a higher authority. In this setting, it is easy to understand how global suffering and severe trauma can crescendo into a global response which culminates in a great religious revolution of united people. Revelation predicts a strong confederation between religious and political leaders will form. (Revelation 13:1-5) In matters of religion, the Roman Catholic Church will provide global leadership since it is internationally respected and presently has official diplomatic ties with 163 nations. No other church on Earth has such prowess.

2. The coming confederation will exert enormous influence and authority over the people of Earth. Due to the chaos caused by the catastrophic events, martial law will be established in most nations. Constitutional rights and privileges, due legal process and other rights which many citizens around the world so freely enjoy today will be nonexistent. In this setting, religious leaders will urge bewildered politicians to create and enforce laws that mandate great respect for God. Religious leaders will forcefully declare that God is justified in His great anger. (What else could they say – that God is *not* justified?) With one voice clergymen from all religious circles will claim that man must repent from his evil ways and honor God with the respect He is due. They will maintain that God's wrath will cease only when repentance and obedience are mandated. "Sinful behavior cannot be tolerated or we will all perish," they will claim. So, religious leaders will seek and obtain laws *mandating* that people stop sinning and worship God. To make their demands effective, they will be sure that severe punishment awaits anyone who refuses to give God respect.

3. Some people will refuse to obey the religious confederation for two reasons. First, there will be general disagreement and widespread dispute among the world's citizens with respect to clergy and law makers mandating righteous behavior through law (legislating the worship of God). There are many different religions in the world and people, in general, resent having another man's view of God crammed down their throat. But, with the smoldering evidences of extensive destruction everywhere, government leaders will

be looking for expedient ways to restore order and they will capitulate to the demands of religious leaders. The overwhelming evidence of destruction everywhere will be a powerful argument that no one should offend God further. Therefore, political leaders will impose "religious" laws upon their citizens to solve the great dilemma of God's wrath. New laws will void a number of basic freedoms, including the privilege to worship God according to the dictates of conscience.

The second type of conflict will become more abrasive and powerful than the first type, because 144,000 "Holy Spirit-filled" people will clearly stand in direct opposition to the religious and political leaders of Babylon. These people will be antagonistic toward everything that the religious confederation represents. Indeed, these individuals will openly and defiantly confront the leaders of the world confederation because they will be God's messengers. Their mission will be threefold: First, they will correctly explain *why* God is doing what He is doing. Second, they will explain *how* God is to be correctly worshiped, which incidently, will be contrary to the laws that religious leaders and politicians have implemented. And third, they will encourage everyone to stand on God's side and *rebel* against the man-made laws which are contrary to the laws of God. The 144,000 will proclaim that people who obey the laws of the confederation will be worshiping the devil himself, instead of God. (Revelation 13:4) Obviously, everyone will be listening, observing and considering this worldwide confrontation. It will prove to be a most interesting controversy.

The Bible Speaks

Some of the information presented in this introduction to Revelation's story should not surprise readers. Scientists and astronomers have been warning world governments for more than ten years that Earth is due a number of catastrophic events, including earthquakes, asteroid impacts, weather changes and volcano eruptions. However, scientists and astronomers lack the insight to predict the human response to these catastrophic events. Fortunately, the book of Revelation tells the whole story. It predicts the physical aspects of the destruction, as well as the human response. Even more important, the book of Revelation reveals the purposes and plans of God and explains why God must do the things that He has chosen to do. The great theme of Revelation's story is man's great need of a Savior. This is why the book's introduction begins with, **"The Revelation of Jesus Christ."** (Revelation 1:1)

Why this Book was Written

The book of Revelation was written for a simple reason: People need to know about coming events. I am not referring to man-made events, but of God's coming judgments. People need to know *what* God is about to do, they need to know *why* and they need to know *now.*

The Bible predicts that God is going to initiate a sequence of 14 events with devastating consequences on the Earth. Remember, these coming events do not happen by chance, for Revelation clearly reveals their specific order. After the seven trumpets begin, billions of people will recognize – sooner or later – that these events are not random convulsions of nature. Rather, all people will eventually recognize them as "Acts of God."

The Bible indicates that God will accomplish four important objectives during the Great Tribulation. First, every person on Earth will be made aware that Jesus, the Judge of all mankind, is about to appear and require an account of each person's behavior. Second, God will expose the properties of sin to the fullest. Few people recognize or understand the powerful, evil effect of sin. Third, God will expose the contents of each human heart. He will give a comprehensive test of faith to each member of the human race. Finally, God will silence the blasphemous claims of the world's religious systems. He will demonstrate that salvation cannot be obtained through membership in *any* religious system. God is about to inform the world that salvation comes only through total commitment and submission to Jesus Christ.

I find that most of the prophetic interpretations we hear on radio and TV are misleading. Do not misunderstand. People can believe anything they choose to believe about the future. However, what a person chooses to believe or not believe has no bearing on coming events. Almost everyone in Noah's day refused to believe a flood was coming. What effect did their denial have on the promised event? My point is that millions of people have been led to anticipate things that will never happen and when the predicted events of Revelation begin, everything that can be shaken, will be shaken. When that day arrives, many people will abandon their faith in God because their ministers misled them; even worse, pastors have failed to spiritually prepare their flocks for the trying circumstances ahead. What is more devastating than the bitter experience of misplaced trust? I address this matter because most ministers, the *trusted* shepherds of the flock, have not honestly considered the coming events or they deny the seriousness of the 14 events that are just before us.

So, Who is Right?

A person might conclude that I have no respect for long-established and well-respected experts on prophecy. Although my assertions may be bold, my comments are not directed at any individual or denomination. (I do not represent nor belong to a denomination.) Nevertheless, it is my conviction that most prophetic teaching is wrong and misleading. I am often scolded for presenting prophetic ideas "that do not respect long established concepts of interpretation." In fact, a few years ago, a preacher scolded me saying, "And who do you think you are? Do you think that God would leap-frog His established agencies of higher learning and dedicated Christian scholars to give *you* special prophetic understanding?"

In the fields of physics, medicine, electronics, engineering and chemistry, it is highly unlikely that an ordinary person can make a significant discovery. However, in the case of prophetic discovery, educational qualifications are not nearly as important as living at the right time. Through the guidance of the Holy Spirit, a person can discover more in 10 minutes than he could learn on his own in 10 years. We live near the end of the world and this is an asset that previous generations of prophetic students did not have. Today, we have access to a wealth of resources and information not previously available. We stand on higher ground. Our view of the past and the oncoming future is clearer because it is now possible to determine our chronological position within apocalyptic prophecy. In addition to this, history confirms a profound point about prophetic study: *Prophetic things are only understood on or about the time of fulfillment.* This principle is true because God only reveals what He wants people to know *when the time* for understanding arrives. So, if anything contributes to a clearer understanding of Bible prophecy today, it is this: There is an end to this world (Revelation 22:12) and **we are the last generation.** The book of Daniel was sealed until the time of the end. (Daniel 12:4,9) If we are near the appointed time of the end, shouldn't we anticipate increased prophetic understanding regarding the coming events and their fulfillment? Indeed, this has been my experience.

The Ultimate Test

No prophetic expositor can prove his or her predictions about the future. It is impossible to prove the truthfulness of a conclusion before it happens. However, there are two ways to test a prediction for accuracy. The most direct method is to document prophetic conclusions before the predicted event comes to pass. Then, when the predicted event occurs, ordinary people can judge the accuracy of the prediction. This simple procedure allows an impartial jury of observers to decide which predictions and interpretations are accurate by simply noting the presence or absence of events which have been predicted.

The second way to verify the truthfulness of a prediction is to use a valid set of rules for interpretation that are "self evident" within the Bible. For example, in the case of apocalyptic prophecy, if a person can demonstrate a previous fulfillment of prophecy, using well-defined rules of interpretation, then his or her interpretation of future prophecies should be consistent with the rules that prove past fulfillments to be true. This demonstration is the only means to avoid a mere human opinion. Of course, the use of valid rules does not prove a prediction to be true, we still have to watch and wait for fulfillment. However, our prophetic views must (1) remain consistent with all that history confirms, and (2) remain consistent with rules that history confirms to be true.

My predictions about coming events are quite different from all the others I have heard. I never intended to be different. I never intended to be a prophetic expositor. Yet, as I struggled to understand the prophecies of Daniel and Revelation for myself, I discovered a simple, but profound truth and this discovery has changed my life.

A Calamity Howler

In March 1991, I concluded that the calamitous events predicted in Revelation could begin during or *after* 1994. Obviously, 1994 has long since passed and my anticipation has proven to be premature. However, understand that my prophetic conclusions have not changed because 1994 has passed, nor have my conclusions been adjusted to incorporate a new timing scheme. Many people misunderstood my interest and emphasis concerning 1994. Perhaps, a better explanation can be given in this edition since my views can no longer be confused with date-setting. See the Appendix for an explanation about the significance of 1994.

This edition (the sixth) has been refined and reduced a few pages, but the message has not been diluted. Rather, it has been concentrated to give you a quicker understanding of the big picture. My goal is not to convince you, but to introduce you to a story that is about to begin – a story that will affect you and me. If, during the coming tribulation, we understand God's plans and purposes, hope will surface and sustain us through Earth's darkest hour. Remember, no matter how dark the night or how extreme our needs, God is always present. God understands our situation. He knows our fears. He will not forsake His children.

Contrary to what many have said, I am not a prophet or a seer. I have not had visions or supernatural encounters with God. I am an ordinary person who has carefully searched the Scriptures to find understanding. I believe God has granted me the desire of my heart – an understanding of Revelation's story. Some people believe I am deluded, but I can truthfully say that I have found the Bible to be **"a lamp unto my feet and a light unto my path."** The Bible is a book without compare and I consider it to be my most valuable possession.

My Findings

I have found 18 prophecies in the books of Daniel and Revelation *and each prophecy behaves in a very consistent manner.* The events in each prophecy are presented in chronological order and they interlink with each other forming a very solid matrix! The key to understanding the 18 mysterious prophecies of Daniel and Revelation came when I discovered four rules of interpretation that bonds each prophecy to the remaining prophecies. Because of this simple discovery, I believe I have stumbled, by the grace of God and the ministry of the Holy Spirit, across a comprehensive and harmonious explanation of the elements in Daniel and Revelation.

Listen to the Holy Spirit

Because of the brevity of this book, I am limited to a condensed discussion about the rules of interpretation (hermeneutics) that support my conclusions. The primary purpose of this book is to introduce you to the discoveries I have found in Daniel and Revelation. If, after reading this book, you want to obtain a deeper understanding of how these conclusions are reached, a list of materials is provided on the final pages of this book.

So, if you read this book before the predicted events begin, and if the Holy Spirit impresses you with the importance of this message, then you have a good reason to share this book with others. If you do not find this message to be true or valuable, then pitch this book into the trash. However, let me caution you regarding one area of prophetic study. Do not displace the voice of the Holy Spirit with the opinions of "experts," employers, friends or family members. Study the message for yourself and listen for God to speak to you. Then decide if this matter is important.

Understanding the Design

Everything in the physical world is governed by laws of design. Laws control the movement of electrons, the effects of gravity, the orbits of planets, and the behavior of all chemical substances. So, as I studied God's Word, I wondered if laws of design also governed the prophecies of Daniel and Revelation in a similar manner. To my amazement, I discovered that they do. In other words, when God gave the prophecies to Daniel and John long ago, He followed a specific design or set of rules. Once we understand His design, we can correctly interpret Daniel and Revelation! I am convinced that God sealed up the knowledge of these laws of design until the end of time was near. In fact, the Bible says twice that the book of Daniel was sealed up until *the time of the end.* (Daniel 12:4,9) These two verses confirm this point: The *only* generation that will correctly understand the prophecies of Daniel will be the *last* generation. The unsealing of Daniel is important because the book of Daniel reveals the laws of design which are also used in Revelation, helping us to accurately interpret Revelation. Remember, the truth about Daniel and Revelation will only be understood at the time of the end.

Since this is a small book, I will get right to the point. I have found four laws of design that consistently operate within the prophecies of Daniel and Revelation. Please understand, I did not make up these four laws – no more than Sir Isaac Newton made up the law of gravity. Rather, I have *observed* four consistent behaviors in the 18 prophecies of Daniel and Revelation. Since I find these behaviors to be consistent, these must be laws of design. Here are the four laws, as described in my words:

Rules of Apocalyptic Interpretation

1. Apocalyptic prophecy is defined as prophecy found in Daniel and Revelation that covers a span of time. Each apocalyptic prophecy has a beginning and ending point in time, and the elements within each apocalyptic prophecy occur in the order they are given.

2. A fulfillment of apocalyptic prophecy occurs when *all* the specifications of the prophecy are met. This includes the chronological order of the elements within the prophecy.

3. Apocalyptic prophecy uses three types of language: Literal, analogous and symbolic. To reach the intended meaning of a given verse, one must: (a) carefully consider the context, (b) if possible, compare the verse with parallel language used in other books of the Bible, (c) if an element is believed to be symbolic, the Bible will clearly interpret the meaning of the symbol with local (highly relevant) Scripture.

4. The operation of the Jubilee Calendar explains when apocalyptic time-periods are to be interpreted as a day for a year or when prophetic time is to be reckoned as literal time.

These laws of design are very important and they reveal why my conclusions presented in this book are so different from the popular ideas being taught on prophecy today. The concept of interpreting prophecy according to laws of design is a crucial matter to me. If there are no laws of design, then diversity of interpretation can be the only result. One Bible scholar may say prophecy means one thing while another, holding the same credentials, may say it means something else. Without rules or knowledge of the master design, how can an ordinary person know what is true and what is false?

When it comes to truth regarding prophecy, religious affiliation should not matter. Whether one is Catholic, Protestant, Jew or Atheist, the truth about coming events will be seen by all. The Bible means what it says, and says what it means. Apocalyptic prophecy was given to man on the basis of what will happen instead of what might have been. So, in the final analysis, prophetic truth is not, nor has it ever been, dependent on the approval or even the understanding of man.

If the process of interpretation is harmonious with the laws of design that God used when constructing the prophecies, nothing can prevent us from reaching a correct understanding *before* the predicted events occur. I disdain the process of interpreting Bible prophecy by reading the headlines of a newspaper. Instead, we should be able to read the Bible and *anticipate* events that will be reported in newspapers later.

The net effect is this. If my understanding about the four laws of design is correct, then other people, following or observing the same laws, should be able to reach the same conclusions that I have without discussing the prophecies with me. Indeed, this has proven to be the case. At this writing, I have come across a dozen people from various denominations (and continents) who have come to similar conclusions. This has been very encouraging since truth is not private or parochial; that is, truth is true everywhere. Truth is universal!

When prophetic expositors fail to understand the laws of design, they must rely on realigning newspaper reports with Bible texts to show some relevancy (or accuracy) for their prophetic claims. This is interpretation by hindsight – "Monday morning quarter-backing." So, the heart of prophetic study boils down to this: Without rules of interpretation, the need for adjustment and validity never ends. Without rules to govern interpretation, prophecy is reduced to an art, and prophetic meaning is in the eye of the beholder. Each man's view is just as valid as any other view. In this setting, Bible prophecy is robbed of what God intended it for – even more sadly, it is reduced to nothing but confusion.

Political events can change quickly and those who base their prophetic understanding on newspaper headlines must continually adjust their claims. Since this is the prevailing method of interpretation today, it has become impossible for laymen to nail down a simple, straightforward explanation of what the Bible actually says about the future. Therefore, valid rules of interpretation are essential. Without them, the meaning of prophecy is just a guessing game.

Again, let me emphasize that my prophetic beliefs have nothing to do with future events. Believing that something will happen or denying that something will happen has no effect whatsoever on what will be. How many in Noah's day denied the flood was coming and what effect did their denial have on the promised event?

Prerequisites

To fully appreciate the prophetic conclusions produced by the laws of interpretation, a person should understand five basic doctrines. They are:

1. The worship of God – His sovereign authority

2. The salvation of God – Our faith in His actions tested

3. The sanctuary of God – His process to save man

4. The coming of God – His indignation with sin

5. The soul of man – Our eternal state

These subjects cannot be presented in this small book even though they need to be addressed. For this reason, the reader is encouraged to obtain materials on these subjects offered on the last page of this book.

A Testing Time

Bible prophecy not only explains *how* the end of the world will occur, but it also tells *why* it must occur. Since most prophetic expositors do not anticipate God's dramatic intervention in the affairs of man, they do not understand the coming drama. In addition, most Christians do not anticipate the "test of faith" that each of us must face. In fact, I have a number of friends who believe in a pre-tribulation rapture. They believe the people of God are going to escape the coming tribulation. If they are correct, then Christians have nothing to worry about. But, if the rapture idea is false, then Christians need some "rapture insurance." It is imperative that we have a comprehensive understanding of God's plans and purposes. In God's prophetic outline, I have not been able to find a pre-tribulation rapture in the apocalyptic sequence of events given in Daniel and Revelation. Instead, I find the dragon (the devil) and his global organization (Babylon) are going to make war on the *last* generation of saints. (See Revelation 12:17; 13:7 and Matthew 24:9.)

So, for readers who sincerely believe in a pre-tribulation rapture, I ask you to consider the message in this book anyway – not for the purpose of changing your mind, but for the purpose of becoming acquainted with the events of the coming tribulation. If the passage of time proves me to be wrong about these things, I will be left with one consolation: I have been conscientious – if I had known the truth, I would have studied and worked just as hard.

Futurism and Historicism

There are several schools of thought on Bible prophecy and naturally, the two most popular views are diametrically opposed. They are very well defined and enthusiastically defended by scholars on both sides. The school of thought having the most followers is called futurism, and its origin can be traced back to the late 1500's. The two most prominent teachings of futurism are variations on the rapture and the restoration of the state of Israel. Even though futurism generates a lot of excitement and discussion, its significance will disappear the day God sends the first global earthquake and the meteoric showers of burning hail.

Futurism misses the mark in several areas, but especially regarding two important points. First, as written earlier, I find no Biblical support for a pre-tribulation or mid-tribulation rapture of all the saints. Yes, I have read the texts used to support the claim of a pre/mid-tribulation rapture. But, the *context* does not support the claim – especially within the sequence of apocalyptic prophecy. Unfortunately, I expect that many sincere people will be overwhelmed when the Great Tribulation begins and they discover they are still on Earth. Many will bitterly lament their unprepared state because they were erroneously led to believe they would escape the tribulation. I am afraid that millions will abandon their faith in God because they will be highly disappointed with their church, their leaders, and their prophetic faith. This, of course, will make the devil very happy. When God's judgments begin, they will not know what or whom to believe.

Second, futurism does not recognize the supreme deception of all ages that is about to take place. The Bible states that the devil *himself* will appear in a physical body all around the Earth. In other words, futurists do not emphasize the brilliant appearing of the devil masquerading as Jesus Christ since they believe they will be raptured (2 Thessalonians 2:3-4). Yes, it's true – Satan, in the radiant form of a God-man, will work mighty miracles. He will even call fire down out of heaven in full view of enormous crowds. (Revelation 13:13) Billions will believe he is Almighty God when, in reality, he is that ancient serpent, the predicted Antichrist. This is a very serious flaw with futurism.

On the other hand, the older and less accepted school of prophetic thought is called historicism. Historicists maintain that the papacy is the great Antichrist power of Daniel and Revelation. This doctrine was developed in England during the 1300's when John Wycliff began to call for reformation within the Roman Catholic Church. Wycliff's clarion call for the exaltation of Bible truth and the elimination of man-made doctrines angered prelates and popes for years. Wycliff did not know that his call for fidelity to Bible truth would culminate with the Protestant Reformation in the 18th century. The problem with historicism today is that it is still bashing the pope and the Roman Catholic Church as though the 18th century reformation was still going on.

Historicists fail to recognize that the world is also made up of other religious systems comprising billions of people. Admittedly, no religious system on Earth today can equal the Roman Catholic Church in political influence; however, there are other religious systems that deviate from Bible truth just as much as papal doctrine. In fact, two religious systems have an even larger number of devoted subjects!

Two major problems exist with the historical view of Revelation: First, historicism teaches that the bulk of Revelation has been fulfilled. Consequently, disciples of this doctrine do not anticipate that the prophecies of Revelation will be fulfilled soon. Since they believe that Revelation, for the most part, has been fulfilled, historicists will experience the same shock that futurists experience when Revelation turns out quite differently than expected!

The second problem deals with Revelation 13. Historicists teach that the seven-headed, ten-horned beast of Revelation 13 is the Roman Catholic Church, and its partner, the lamb-like beast, is the United States of America. These two powers, they believe, will rule over *all the inhabitants of the Earth* and set up the mark of the beast. Yes, the papacy and the United States will be major players during end-time events, but they will not be the only players! This world is made up of many political and religious systems and Revelation's story not only identifies many of them, it includes them all.

Opposite Views Produce the Same Effect

Both futurism and historicism, even though diametrically opposed to each other, produce the same erroneous conclusion. Futurists plan to be in Heaven while Revelation is being fulfilled, and historicists are convinced that most of Revelation has already happened! The bottom line from both schools of thought is that understanding the details of Revelation is not *essential*!

God's Silence

God *appears* to be silent because He has not openly interfered with the actions of man for many centuries. However, God is going to break His long-standing silence with our planet by sending His judgments. These judgments will come from the heavens, as well as from deep within the Earth. When they begin, sinners will know that "The Great Day of the Lord" has come. It will be clear to all people that God is dealing with the sinfulness of Earth's inhabitants. In days to come, everyone will experience the fear of Almighty God. I know this sounds like a fairy tale, but soon, perhaps 30-60 days after the first global earthquake, I expect to see the formation of a powerful religious confederation that involves all the religious leaders of Earth. Even as religious leaders convene to form the confederation, martial laws will be implemented in all nations almost immediately. When that day arrives, the leaders of Earth will unwittingly begin to fulfill prophecies that were written more than two thousand years ago.

I am excited about the nearness of these events because I see that the stage is *now* set. End-time players are in place. World leaders are seeking peace and unity – a one-world coalition of nations governed by international law. World leaders say they want peace and safety for all people, but progress is slow. The basic problem is this: The heart of man is selfish. Greed, arrogance and pride are at the root of madness, war and unrest. But, the coming judgments of God will change the political structures of the world overnight. God is about to transfer control of the world to the Antichrist, the leaders of seven religious systems, and ten political leaders – eighteen players total. God will test the inhabitants of the world to see who loves Him supremely. The world's leaders do not know it yet, but God has planned this for thousands of years.

As you read this little book, keep in mind that the Bible underscores a glorious, but sublime truth. God does not condemn a person for believing a lie. Rather, He only condemns those who willfully refuse to believe the truth! (James 4:17) Think of it this way. If God places the clearest evidences of truth before His creatures and they refuse to agree with principles of righteousness, what more can He do? Would you want someone in your eternal kingdom who refuses to love what is righteous? Is life – whose source is God – a privilege or a right? Are rebellious creatures just as deserving of eternal life as submissive creatures? Where in this universe can a rebellious creature live in peace if God is omnipresent throughout His realm? These are thoughtful questions that each of us should consider. The coming Kingdom of Heaven has a set of issues and considerations that go far beyond our brief life span of 70 years and the limits of travel we have today.

It is time to end this lengthy, but essential introduction. If my conclusions are right, we are about to see the day when God breaks His silence. On that dreadful day, everyone will know that God's patience with sin and sinners has reached its limit. On that day, mortals on a tiny speck of a planet called Earth will know that Almighty God, Owner of the Universe, has summoned man to rendezvous before His everlasting throne of righteousness.

Larry Wilson

June, 1997

Chapter 2
The Full Cup Principle

God Largely Misunderstood Today

The character of God is poorly understood throughout the world. Most men and women do not appreciate His love, authority, glory and power because He has not openly revealed Himself in the affairs of man in recent times. However, God allowed Isaiah to see His omnipotence. Isaiah was amazed at God's reluctance to show Himself as the Almighty. Isaiah wrote, **"Truly you are a God who hides himself, O God and Savior of Israel."** (Isaiah 45:15)

God's *apparent* silence comes as a consequence of sin. Just as offenses physically separate friends or family members, the offensiveness of sin has separated us from God's physical presence. As generations come and go, the knowledge of God dims. The reality of God becomes faint, and the longer we go without renewed evidence of God's authority and glory, the more silent He appears to be. In the vacuum of this silence, sin becomes more attractive and less offensive. Sinners become bold and defiant in transgression. Violence, sorrow and suffering spring up like dandelions after a spring rain. Every night, the evening news confirms our rapid slide into depravity. Degenerate, even hideous sins are either glamorized, justified or treated as inconsequential on TV. Sin has a strange effect on human beings – it causes sinners to minimize the effects or the guilt of their wrong doing. Think about this for a full two seconds: Sin causes human beings to either justify or deflect the responsibility of wrong doing! (How many in prison falsely maintain their innocence?) Hasn't this been apparent from the beginning? Didn't Adam and Eve justify or deflect responsibility for their sin in the Garden of Eden? (Genesis 3:12,13)

God is Not Forever Silent

The Bible confirms that God breaks His silence from time to time by using His four judgments to limit the growth of sin. (Ezekiel 14:21) His four judgments are sword, famine, plague and wild beasts. In His infinite wisdom, God allows nations to rule until they fill up their cup of iniquity, and when they do, the Bible says He removes them from power. (See Daniel 2:21; 4:17; Leviticus 18:24-28.) What makes this process so remarkable is that God, even within the chaos of sin, completely accomplishes His plans and purposes on this Earth! We may try to explain the outcome of earthly events by analyzing the actions of the players, but this is only a limited view. Do not be naive and think that things just happen by the prowess of man. Nothing happens in the universe without God's knowledge and permission. Even though we are not able to see God on His throne, we can know He reigns over the kingdoms of man. God is sovereign. We may not see all that He is doing, but the evidence is right before our eyes. The Bible is clear. God is in control. How He maintains control is a mystery. That He does it without showing Himself is His silence.

God's silence is not too hard to penetrate if you really want to see and hear Him. The evidences of His handiwork are all around us if we want to acknowledge Him. However, if we choose not to give Him respect, we can easily ignore Him and deny the recognition He is due. Thus, His silence complements our power of choice. God can either be the greatest and most wonderful Being in the universe, or if we so choose, we can deny His existence. What a God! Perhaps the least understood element within God's character is His reluctance to awe His creatures with His power and presence. His silence will be a topic of eternal discovery!

Very Important Point

When God breaks His silence by raining down judgments on Earth, the events will be comprehended even though God's purposes will be grossly misunderstood. To appease God and stop His awful judgments and wrath, the world's population, and especially its religious leaders, will encourage politicians to enact laws "honoring and appeasing the God of Heaven." However, mandating righteousness (the enforcement of laws requiring the exaltation of God) will be contrary to what He actually wants! What God wants from man – has always wanted from man – is a repentant heart and a submissive attitude. He wants men and women to recognize His sovereignty, not for who He is, but for what

He is and what He represents. He calls men and women to live a life free of the damning power of sin. Even more, He will grant everyone who sincerely desires, the power to be victorious over sin and our natural rebellion against Him. However, Revelation predicts that the majority of men and women will reject God's terms and conditions for salvation. Hardened by life-long rebellion, the hearts of many people are so numbed by sin that even God cannot reach them. Think of man's coming foolishness. How can mandated righteousness produce a broken heart and a repentant spirit?

Revelation describes how wicked people will be filled with a spirit of hatred when confronted with the truth about God and His will. This confrontation will be initiated when God selects and anoints 144,000 servant-prophets to speak on His behalf. These spirit-filled people will speak to the inhabitants of every nation. Evil men will punish and torture God's servants because their message will disclose man's rebellion against God. God's messengers will be in direct conflict with those who govern a world that currently belongs to Satan. (Luke 4:5-6) The persecutors will think, like Pilate, that they can wash their hands from the guilt of these acts. Yet, God *never* ignores evil, even though He may allow it to flourish for a season. God will avenge completely every evil deed and will see that people receive double the pain in return for the pain they inflicted. (See Revelation 18:6, 2 Corinthians 5:10 and Obadiah 1:15.)

In the context of His coming judgments, God's character and His behavior will be misrepresented and misinterpreted.

This is the heart of Revelation's story. It is a story of a patient God visiting a planet in deep trouble. It is also a story about rebellious people and a world gone astray. Most people, when put to the coming test, will openly and willfully reject the clearest evidences of God's truth and God's sovereignty. They will unite themselves in rebellion against the laws of the Most High God by obeying the laws of the coming glorious man-God, the Antichrist – the devil himself. God is going to allow Satan to physically appear all over the world because **"they refused to love the truth and so be saved."** (2 Thessalonians 2:10-11) Jesus said, **"This is the verdict: Light has come into the world, but men loved darkness instead of light because their deeds were evil. Everyone who does evil hates the light, and will not come into the light for fear that his deeds will be exposed."** (John 3:19-20)

God's Wrath

Let us put God's wrath into perspective. Bible history reveals that God follows a consistent principle in dealing with humanity. I call this principle the "full cup principle." The concept is so simple that a child can understand it. In essence, when a person, city, nation or body of people reach a certain level of decadence or wickedness, God's patience expires and He breaks His silence by using one or more of His divine judgments. If the situation is redeemable, His judgments are redemptive. If the situation is beyond redemption, His judgments are destructive. In fact, the coming events predicted in Revelation are divided into two groups of seven.

The first seven plagues (seven trumpets) are redemptive. The seven last plagues (seven bowls) are destructive.

Many people currently interpret God's silence or passiveness with evil to mean that He is either nonexistent or indifferent to what we do. Others see His permissiveness as proof that He is not interested in each person's day-to-day activities. For this reason, a growing number of people are committing horrible evil deeds, thinking that God does not see them nor will He hold each of them responsible for their actions. The truth is that many people do not realize the strict accountability we must each give to God for every action! Solomon said, **"Now all has been heard; here is the conclusion of the matter: Fear God and keep his commandments, for this is the whole duty of man. For God will bring every deed into judgment, including every hidden thing, whether it is good or evil."** (Ecclesiastes 12:13,14)

Examples of the Full Cup Principle

The antediluvians filled up their cup: **"The Lord saw how great man's wickedness on the Earth had become, and that every inclination of the thoughts of his heart was only evil all the time. The Lord was grieved that he had made man on the Earth, and his heart was filled with pain. So the Lord said, 'I will wipe mankind, whom I have created, from the face of the Earth – men and animals, and creatures that move along the ground, and birds of the air – for I am grieved that I have made them.' "** (Genesis 6:5-7) God destroyed the world with a flood in Noah's day because the antediluvians' cup of iniquity had reached full measure. God broke His silence using Noah to warn the world about what He was going to do. Then, as promised, He destroyed the inhabitants of the world. When divine love and mercy no longer produce repentance and reformation, as with the antediluvians, God's justice demands destructive action.

The Amorites filled their cup: **"Then the Lord said to him (Abraham), 'Know for certain that your descendants will be strangers in a country not their own, and they will be enslaved and mistreated four hundred years. But I will punish the nation they serve as slaves, and afterward they will come out with great possessions. You, however, will go to your fathers in peace and be buried at a good old age. In the fourth generation your descendants will come back here, for the sin of the Amorites has not yet reached its full measure.'"** (Genesis 15:13-16)

Notice the last sentence of the previous text. God would give Canaan to Abraham's offspring only *after* the sins of the Amorites had reached full measure! Make no mistake about this. Canaan belongs to the Creator, and He would give Canaan to Abraham's descendants only *after* the Amorites had exhausted their chance for possessing that beautiful land. Keep in mind that ancient Israel's possession of Canaan was based on the *same* conditions that applied to the Amorites. Moses knew that Israel's possession of Canaan was conditional. So, he warned Israel: **"But be assured today that the Lord your God is the one who goes across** ahead of you like a devouring fire. He will destroy them; he will subdue them before you. And you will drive them out and annihilate them quickly ... After the Lord your God has driven them out before you, do not say to yourself, 'The Lord has brought me here to take possession of this land because of my righteousness.' No, it is on account of the wickedness of these nations that the Lord is going to drive them out before you. It is not because of your righteousness or your integrity that you are going in to take possession of their land; but on account of the wickedness of these nations . . . ." (Deuteronomy 9:3-5) This is an extremely important point: The Canaanites were also driven out and/or destroyed when they filled their cup of wickedness! When God's patience with the Canaanites reached its limit, He broke His silence by sending His wrath upon them! (Leviticus 18:24-25)

Eventually, Israel filled its cup: Just before the Babylonian captivity (605 B.C.), God told Israel, **"But you did not listen to me . . . and you have provoked me with what your hands have made, and you have brought harm to yourselves ... Because you have not listened to my words, I will summon all the peoples of the north and my servant Nebuchadnezzar king of Babylon . . . and I will bring them against this land and its inhabitants and against all the surrounding nations. I will completely destroy them and make them an object of horror and scorn, and an everlasting ruin . . . This whole country will become a desolate wasteland, and these nations will serve the king of Babylon seventy years. But when the** seventy years are fulfilled, I will punish the king of Babylon and his nation, the land of the Babylonians, for their guilt ... and will make it desolate forever." (Jeremiah 25:7-12)

Notice this: According to the text, Israel was destroyed for provoking God, *and* the prophecy also includes the punishment of pagan Babylon! This proves that God deals with the heathen just as He deals with those who know Him! In God's eyes, wickedness is wickedness. Each person, city, nation and kingdom has a cup and when it becomes full, God breaks His silence.

Another point about ancient Babylon must be made. When the mysterious handwriting appeared on the palace wall, Belshazzar, King of Babylon, suspected that God was sending the sword against him, so he summoned the prophet Daniel to interpret the handwriting. Before giving the interpretation, Daniel recounted the divine judgments that God had sent upon his arrogant grandfather, Nebuchadnezzar. Then Daniel said, **"But you his son, O Belshazzar, have not humbled yourself, though you knew all this. Instead, you have set yourself up against the Lord of heaven ... But you did not honor the God who holds in his hand your life and all your ways ... This is what these words mean: *Mene*: God has numbered the days of your reign and brought it to an end. *Tekel*: You have been weighed on the scales and found wanting. *Peres*: Your kingdom is divided and given to the Medes and Persians."** (Daniel 5:22-28) As written earlier, the reason Revelation calls the coming religious coalition, Babylon, is that its character will parallel the arrogant and rebellious character of ancient Babylon.

New Testament Examples

The full cup principle concept is also in the New Testament. Paul warned the sexually immoral Romans, ". . . you are storing up wrath against yourself for the day of God's wrath, when his righteous judgment will be revealed. God will give to each person according to what he has done. But for those who are self-seeking and who reject the truth and follow evil, there will be wrath and anger." (Romans 2:5,6,8) Compare these verses with Paul's statement in 2 Corinthians 5:10: "For we must all appear before the judgment seat of Christ, that each one may receive what is due him for the things done while in the body, whether good or bad." Paul understood why God's wrath is coming. He told the believers in Colosse, "Put to death, therefore, whatever belongs to your earthly nature: sexual immorality, impurity, lust, evil desires and greed, which is idolatry. Because of these, the wrath of God is coming." (Colossians 3:5,6)

Paul encouraged the believers in Thessalonica to be patient in their suffering until the enemies of Christ had filled up their cup. ". . . You suffered from your own countrymen the same things those churches (in Judea) suffered from the Jews, who killed the Lord Jesus and the prophets and also drove us out. They (the Jews) displease God and are hostile to all men in their effort to keep us from speaking to the Gentiles so that they may be saved. In this way they always heap up their sins to the limit. The wrath of God has come upon them at last." (1 Thessalonians 2:14-16) When Paul wrote this epistle, he knew the Jewish nation had filled its cup and that the Romans were going to destroy it. Rome destroyed Jerusalem in A.D. 70 just as Christ prophesied. (Luke 21:22)

Jesus Condemns the Jewish Nation Using the Full Cup Principle

Jesus explained the full cup principle in a discourse with the Pharisees. After pronouncing seven curses on the Jewish leaders for their religious bigotry and hypocrisy, Jesus said, **"Fill up, then, the measure of the [cup of] sin of your forefathers! You snakes! You brood of vipers! How will you escape being condemned to hell? (Matthew 23:32,33)** Again, the point is made. When a nation or individual reaches the limit of divine forbearance, God breaks His silence. His mercy with sin and sinners has a limit. Jesus concluded His denunciation of the Jewish nation by saying, **"O Jerusalem, Jerusalem, you who kill the prophets and stone those sent to you, how often I have longed to gather your children together, as a hen gathers her chicks under her wings, but you were not willing. Look, your house is left to you desolate."** (Matthew 23:37,38) Later, Jesus predicted Jerusalem's destruction *as a fulfillment* of God's wrath: **"When you see Jerusalem being surrounded by armies, you will know that its *desolation* is near. Then let those who are in Judea flee to the mountains, let those in the** city get out, and let those in the country not enter the city. For this is the time of punishment in fulfillment of all that has been written [in the Scriptures concerning Israel]." (Luke 21:20-22)

Does God Kill People?

From time to time, scholars and pastors assert that God does not kill or destroy people. They defend this by saying, (1) "God does not violate His own commandment, **'Thou shalt not kill'** and/or (2) "God just steps aside and turns evil people over to the natural consequences of sin which brings death and destruction." The justification used to promote this view of God is false. This position ignores the weight of evidence found throughout the entire Bible and exclusively focuses on only two aspects of God's character. In simple terms, advocates of this view say that God is love. Because He is love, He does not violate His character of love by doing evil (killing). (1 John 4:8) Second, they claim that God would not break His own law; namely, **"Thou shalt not kill."** (Exodus 20:13, KJV) They use these two points to prove that God neither destroys nor kills, but simply steps out of the way when people become totally evil. He either allows sin to take its natural, destructive course or He turns them over to the devil – allowing Satan to do whatever he wishes.

Falsehoods about God's character do a lot of damage when they are partially true. (An effective lie is 99% truth.) True, God is love and He has a wonderful purpose for His creatures. He loves man, works with man, and desires the best for man. However, God requires man to live within certain boundaries – both physical and moral. For example, the law of momentum states: Mass times velocity equals momentum. A 3,000 pound car doing 60 miles-per-hour has a lot of momentum. Suppose the driver gets drunk and his car hits a concrete object and as a result, the driver dies. Did God kill the driver? No. The law of momentum did. So, there is validity to the claim that sin has its consequences. But the question remains, did a loving God create the law of momentum that killed the drunk driver? Yes, God created the law of momentum and He wants us to respect His laws. However, if a person chooses to get drunk and violates the law of momentum, we would have to conclude that the drunk essentially killed himself.

What about the sixth commandment, **"Thou shalt not kill?"** Does God violate His own commandment and kill people? As we examine this question closely, it is imperative that we understand the intent of the **"Thou shalt not kill"** commandment. Within God's rules for life, there are a few occasions where death can be inflicted (capital punishment) *without breaking* God's law. Notice what the Lord told Noah on his exit from the ark: **"And for your lifeblood I will surely demand an accounting. I will demand an accounting from every animal. And from each man, too, I will demand an accounting for the life of his fellow man. Whoever sheds the blood of man, by man shall his blood be shed; for in the image of God has God made man."** (Genesis 9:5,6) This verse shows that God commanded murderers to be put to death by other men. Capital punishment is not man's invention. The Bible reveals that capital punishment originated in the mind of God – not man. (See also Leviticus 20.)

In the wilderness, God not only spoke the Ten Commandments to the children of Israel, He also elaborated more fully on the terms and conditions for capital punishment. **"These are to be legal requirements for you throughout the generations to come, wherever you live. Anyone who kills a person is to be put to death as a murderer only on the testimony of witnesses. But no one is to be put to death on the testimony of only one witness. Do not accept a ransom for the life of a murderer, who deserves to die. He must surely be put to death."** (Numbers 35:29-31)

The point is that God does not break His own law by requiring men to put murderers to death. A person has to incorporate *all* that God has said about killing to understand His *intent* for the laws that govern life and death. So, people who claim that God cannot kill because He will not break His own law do not understand the intent of the Ten Commandments! When God said, **"Thou shalt not kill,"** He commanded individuals not to commit premeditated murder. However, if someone chooses to commit murder, God declares that the murderer must be put to death and the next of kin can kill the murderer *without incurring guilt.* Notice, **"[If] the avenger of blood finds him** [the murderer] **outside the city** [of refuge]**, the avenger of blood may kill the accused without being guilty of murder."** (Numbers 35:27) If sinful man can kill without incurring guilt under lawful circumstances, so can God.

Underlying Principle

The underlying principles behind capital punishment are atonement and restitution. God requires atonement and restitution for every sin. In God's order, there is no forgiveness for sin. Now, before you jump to any hasty conclusions, keep on reading. I am not saying that *sinners* are not forgiven. I am saying that *sin* itself is not forgiven. At first, this statement seems contradictory, but this is what atonement is all about. Atonement for sin is possible only after restitution has been made. This is why Jesus died on the cross. God placed the sins of man upon Christ and He was slain for our sins. We may say that our sins are forgiven, but this is not the whole story. The sins of believers can be transferred to Jesus because He atoned for our sins by shedding His blood. He is our atonement. If the Old Testament sanctuary service teaches us anything, it is this: God requires atonement for all wrong doing. **"For the life of a creature is in the blood, and I have given it to you to make atonement for yourselves on the altar; it is the blood that makes atonement for one's life."** (Leviticus 17:11) **"In fact, the law requires that nearly everything be cleansed with blood, and without the shedding of blood there is no forgiveness."** (Hebrews 9:22)

Individuals who claim that God does not kill people cannot give a reason for the death of the firstborn, both men and animals, at the time of the Exodus. The Lord warned Moses that if the destroying angel did not find blood on the doorposts, *He* Himself would slay the firstborn of each family, whether man or animal! **"On that same night *I* will pass through Egypt and strike down every firstborn – both men and animals – and *I* will bring judgment on all the gods of Egypt. *I am the Lord.*"** (Exodus 12:12, italics mine)

This is an important point. Who claims responsibility for killing the eldest (the highest ranking) family member of men and animals in Egypt? Who spoke to Moses? If we make the devil responsible, then we must conclude that (1) the devil is speaking in Exodus 12, or (2) God and the devil were partners in the killing. However, God does not *use* the devil to accomplish works of righteousness. Furthermore, if God simply turned His back on the firstborn in Egypt and *allowed* the devil to kill this select group of people, then God would be an accomplice to murder. (God says that if an individual has the opportunity to prevent harm and does nothing about it, he becomes an accomplice to the harm committed and shares in its guilt. (Ezekiel 3:17-21) But, the real point here is, do we take God at His word? Does God claim that He kills people? Notice what the Lord told Moses: **"See now that I myself am He! There is no God besides me. I put to death and I bring to life, I have wounded and I will heal, and no one can deliver out of my hand."** (Deuteronomy 32:39)

The deaths of the firstborn in Egypt reveal something important about the character of God. He gave Pharaoh and his court nine plagues to convince them that He was Sovereign, but Pharaoh refused to recognize God's authority. During the Great Tribulation, history will be repeated. Men and women will refuse the commands of the Almighty and they will receive His plagues! When men and women openly rebel against God, what more can He do? What are God's options if individuals willfully refuse to recognize the difference between right and wrong? God killed Egypt's firstborn as an object lesson for Israel and to punish Egypt. Egypt's punishment was due to open rebellion against the authority of God. The object lesson for Israel was even more impressive! The "passing over" pointed forward to a time when God would pass over every human being in judgment to see if the blood of His sacrifice (Jesus) was on the door posts of the heart. (2 Corinthians 5:10) The death of the firstborn in Egypt was a shadow of the death of God's only Son that would be necessary for man's salvation. (The story of Abraham and Isaac reveals the same concept. God tested Abraham's faith to see if Abraham was willing to do to his own son what God would have to do to His Son.) No wonder Jesus is called the Lamb *of God.* (John 1:29)

Incidently, the New Testament describes three instances in which people were killed outright under interesting circumstances. Read Acts 5:1-11 and Acts 12:23 and see if you can determine who did the killing. Also examine 2 Kings 1:1-17 and see who destroyed 102 men with fire. Then read Isaiah 37:36 and see who killed 185,000 men. These texts should help to dismiss any doubt on this compelling subject.

God's Wrath will be Revealed in Our Day

"I the Lord have spoken. The time has come for me to act. I will not hold back; I will not have pity, nor will I relent. You will be judged according to your conduct and your actions, declares the Sovereign Lord." (Ezekiel 24:14) When the Lord spoke these words to Ezekiel, He was indirectly referring to the full cup principle. Our day is coming. God will break His silence and demonstrate His animosity toward sin. It will happen suddenly, severing the past from the oncoming future. Life as we know it will immediately and irrevocably change. The world has never witnessed anything like the coming judgments of God, nor can it sustain more than one visitation. God will act suddenly and powerfully, and all the inhabitants of Earth will be overwhelmed with the swiftness and intensity. In this context, the authority, character and actions of God will become the subject of profound interest and controversy among all the people of Earth.

Fourth Seal is the Next Seal

The first global earthquake will be a signal that Jesus has opened the fourth seal. (Note: The seven seals began to open in 1798. At this time, three have been opened and the fourth is next. This matter is discussed at length in my book, *The Revelation of Jesus*.)

John writes, **"When the Lamb opened the fourth seal... I looked, and there before me was a pale horse! Its rider was named Death, and Hades was following close behind him. They were given power over a fourth of the Earth to kill by sword, famine and plague, and by the wild beasts of the Earth."** (Revelation 6:7,8)

Did you notice the four judgments of sword, famine, plague and wild beasts? So, what is the purpose of the fourth seal and why would the Lamb open this seal and kill 25% of Earth? Isaiah explains: **"See, the Lord is going to lay waste the Earth and devastate it; he will ruin its face and scatter its inhabitants ... The Earth will be completely laid waste and totally plundered. The Lord has spoken this word ... The Earth is defiled by its people; they have disobeyed the laws, violated the statutes and broken the everlasting covenant. Therefore a curse consumes the earth; its people must bear their guilt. Therefore Earth's inhabitants are burned up, and very few are left."** (Isaiah 24:1-6)

Symbolic or Literal – In the Past or Far Into the future?

Some people argue that the four judgments of the fourth seal are symbolic and therefore, not literal events. Others say the fourth seal happened long ago, while still others believe it happens after a rapture. And of course, some people believe that God does not kill anyway, so what is the truth?

We need to let the Bible speak for itself. Consider God's comments to Ezekiel (especially note the words that I have italicized): **"Son of man, if a country sins against *me* by being unfaithful and *I* stretch out my hand against it to cut off its food supply and send famine upon it and *kill* its men and their animals ... Or if *I* send wild beasts through that country and they leave it childless and it becomes desolate so that no one can pass through it because of the beasts ... Or if *I* bring a sword against that** country and say, 'Let the sword pass throughout the land,' and *I kill* its men and their animals . . . Or if *I* send a plague into that land and pour out my wrath upon it through bloodshed, *killing* its men and their animals . . . For this is what the Sovereign Lord says: How much worse will it be when *I* send against Jerusalem *my* four dreadful judgments – sword and famine and wild beasts and plague – to *kill* its men and their animals . . . They will come to you (Ezekiel), and when you see their conduct and their actions, you will be consoled regarding the disaster *I* have brought upon Jerusalem – *every disaster I have brought upon it.* You will be consoled when you see their conduct and their actions, for you will know that *I have done nothing in it without cause*, declares the Sovereign Lord." (Ezekiel 14:13-23)

How can anyone dispute that God's four judgments – plague, famine, sword and wild beasts – are not literal after reading these verses? God's literal judgments kill literal people, and further, God personally claims responsibility for the killing caused by these four judgments. God justified His actions to Ezekiel by saying, "**I have done nothing in it without cause.**" (Ezekiel 14:23) God's character and purposes are far more complex than most people understand. It is plain to see that God has used sword, famine, plague and wild beasts in the past and He is going to use His four judgments again. They are specifically mentioned in the fourth seal. These judgments will be sent upon the whole Earth at the end-time for one purpose – Earth's cup of iniquity is full.

Bible History is Clear

The Bible explains how God implements His four judgments. Notice these examples:

Sword: God uses military leaders to execute the sword of His divine will. From Jeremiah 25:9 we learn that God sent His *servant,* King Nebuchadnezzar, against Jerusalem. I find it interesting that Nebuchadnezzar did not know he was a servant of the Most High God at the time! Nevertheless, God used the pagan king to destroy Jerusalem. In the same way, God destroyed the empire of Babylon through Darius, another unwitting servant of God. (Daniel 5:30,31) The Bible also says that King Cyrus was a servant of God. (See Ezra 1:1 and Isaiah 44:28, 25:1.) This concept is especially fascinating since God is able to accomplish His plans without forcing His will on any individual!

Famine: God also sends famine to accomplish His purposes. In Genesis 41, God sent a seven-year famine to Egypt, and in the process, removed Joseph from prison and put him on the throne. This amazing promotion for Joseph opened the way for the descendants of Abraham to move to Egypt! (Genesis 15:12-16)

In 2 Samuel 21:1 the Bible says, **"During the reign of David, there was a famine for three successive years; so David sought the face of the Lord. The Lord said, 'It is on account of Saul and his blood-stained house; it is because he put the Gibeonites to death.'"** Clearly, this three-year famine was the direct result of Saul's disobedience.

In 2 Kings 8:1, we learn of another seven-year famine the Lord sent: **"Now Elisha had said to the woman whose son he had restored to life, 'Go away with your family and stay for a while wherever you can, because the Lord has decreed a famine in the land that will last seven years.' "**

Perhaps one of the best-known famines recorded in the Bible occurred during the days of Elijah and King Ahab. Notice what James says: **"Elijah was a man just like us. He prayed earnestly that it would not rain, and it did not rain on the land for three and a half years. Again he prayed, and the heavens gave rain, and the Earth produced its crops."** (James 5:17,18)

Plague: Plagues can come in numerous forms. We think of bubonic plague or cholera as a plague, but the word *plague* encompasses anything troublesome or afflicting. Here are a few Biblical examples: God sent plagues on Pharaoh and Egypt to convince Pharaoh that He wanted His people set free. These plagues included frogs, water-to-blood, gnats, flies, boils, hail, locusts, darkness, etc. (See Exodus 8-10.) The Lord killed 10 of the 12 spies with a plague for giving a bad report about the Promised Land! (Numbers 14:37) Korah started a rebellion in the wilderness and more than 14,700 people died. (Numbers 16:49) On one occasion, God sent a plague that killed 24,000 people for sexual immorality! (Numbers 25:9) On another occasion, God sent a plague that killed 70,000 Israelites because King David disobeyed the Lord and took a census. (1 Chronicles 21:14-16) Whether we like it or not, God sends plagues to kill people if their evil ways warrant such drastic action! Notice the warning that will be given to the inhabitants of Earth during the Great Tribulation: **". . . 'If anyone worships the beast and his image and receives his mark on the forehead or on the hand, he, too, will drink of the wine of God's fury, which has been poured full strength into the cup of his wrath. He will be tormented with burning sulfur in the presence of the holy angels and of the Lamb.'"** (Revelation 14:9-10) What is this "full strength" potion that has been poured into the cup of God's wrath? Revelation 15:1 says, **" I saw in heaven another great and marvelous sign: seven angels with the seven last plagues—last, because with them God's wrath is completed."**

Wild beasts: Wild beasts, like plagues, come in many forms. Peter described them saying, **"I looked into it** (the sheet) **and saw four-footed animals of the Earth, wild beasts, reptiles, and birds of the air."** (Acts 11:6) Most of the creatures of Earth are considered wild beasts. So, how does God use them? The Lord clearly warned Jeremiah how He would use wild beasts to accomplish His deadly purpose on Israel: **" 'I will send four kinds of destroyers against them (Israel),' declares the Lord, 'the sword to kill and the dogs to drag away and the birds of the air and the beasts of the Earth to devour and destroy.' "** (Jeremiah 15:3) God also sent poisonous vipers into the camp of Israel when they complained and opposed Him. (See Numbers 21:4-9.) One family of "wild beasts" that may be influential in the future is insects. Killer bees, fleas, fire ants, swarms of locusts and other tiny creatures can cause unbelievable damage! God promised Israel that He would restrain the wild beasts if they would repent from their idolatry and love and obey Him. God said, **"I will make a covenant of peace with them (Israel) and rid the land of wild beasts so that they may live in the desert and sleep in the forests in safety."** (Ezekiel 34:25)

Back to the Fourth Seal

Even though God uses His four judgments to deal with people and nations when their cup of sin becomes full, the Bible also reveals that He does so only when sin and rebellion reach a point where His love and mercy have no redeeming effect. (See Ezekiel 5.) So, the judgments described in the fourth seal are literal and should be taken most seriously. Remember, Revelation 6:8 reveals that there is going to be at least 1.5 billion casualties (25% of Earth) as a result of God's judgments! This proves that God is willing to sacrifice a large number of people for the salvation of others. After all, didn't He sacrifice His own Son for the salvation of all? We cannot conceptualize the breadth of God's interest in our salvation without considering the extensive destruction of the fourth seal. To some, this may sound terribly cruel and unfair. However, if the coming of Jesus is delayed another century, all six billion people currently living on Earth will die anyway. By accelerating the death of some people, others will be saved. This is a strange thing to say, but God is left – at times – with no other option but to destroy many to save a few. Remember the flood?

If we consider the severity of the coming judgments that Jesus is going to send upon the Earth, we will get a greater appreciation for the dominion and importance of God's law. Understand that God's wrath is not like human temper. His anger is justified. His coming judgments have a purpose. The seven first plagues are for the saving of mankind. The seven last plagues are reserved to destroy those people who choose to rebel against His authority. Keep in mind that God's judgments are always fair, regardless of when a person dies. Be assured that He will judge those individuals who perish in the forthcoming judgments just as fairly as He judges those who die every day. God is more than fair. He does no wrong. Deuteronomy 32:4 says, **" He is the Rock, his works are perfect, and all his ways are just. A faithful God who does no wrong, upright and just is he."**

One last point needs to be made. God does not see death as we do. After all, He can speak the word and a dead man becomes a living man! (John 11:43) In fact, the Bible says that God considers the dead as though they are *suspended* in time until the resurrection. Consider the following texts and see what you think! (Luke 20:38; Psalm 115:17; Ecclesiastes 9:5,6; John 6:39-54)

If you have an intimate relationship with Jesus Christ and consider Him your Savior, then you have no reason to be afraid of the coming judgments. The Psalmist wrote, **"Even though I walk through the valley of the shadow of death, I will fear no evil, for you are with me . . . ."** (Psalm 23:4) Jesus said: **"If you love me, you will obey what I com-**

mand." (John 14:15) Accept His gift of grace which enables you to obey the teachings of Jesus and live by faith in His promises. Follow the prompting of the Holy Spirit and God will take care of you – even in death. Earth's cup of iniquity is almost full. God is about to break His silence. The end of this old Earth is just before us and the beginning of the New Earth lies just beyond.

Given the contents of this chapter, this statement may sound like a contradiction in terms, but Revelation contains a story about God's desperate love for man. Jesus is anxious to save, but the human race is so blighted by sin that most people cannot understand the character of God or the principles of His Kingdom. However, God will bring before every person's conscience, the reality of His Holy character by sending His judgments. Into this turmoil, He will send 144,000 messengers to explain the terms and conditions of salvation. Yes, He wants everyone to be saved, but many will refuse to listen. Few will give Him the respect He deserves. Hopefully, some people will discover their desperate need of a loving Savior in times of distress. What does it say about the condition of the human race when God is left with no other option but to display His wrath to get our undivided attention?

Chapter 3

God Breaks His Silence with Seven Trumpets

Now that we know *why* God's judgments are coming, we need to understand *how* they come. Revelation predicts a sequence of 14 events before Jesus Christ returns. For people who are willing to compare events with what is clearly written in the Bible, there will be no question that God is doing exactly what He said He would do. God's plans for the coming tribulation can be understood by anyone who sincerely wants to know. If the Bible record about coming events was obscure and mysterious, how could God's children be certain that He is in control when the tribulation begins? Nothing is more powerful than truth whose time has come. This simple point will someday stand in direct opposition to the claims of skeptics. Indeed, you can be sure of this development: Many scientists will at first deny that the judgments are Acts of God. Instead, they will say that these calamities are just nature's random curse. On the other hand, leaders of the worldwide religious coalition (Babylon) will claim that these events are judgments of God. However, instead of obeying God's laws, they will impose man-made laws contrary to the law of God. What a time of coming confusion!

A Great Earthquake

The first physical sign that the Great Tribulation has begun will be a global earthquake that will shake the whole world. (**Note:** This earthquake (Revelation 8:5) is the first of four earthquakes predicted in Revelation.) This first earthquake will signal the end of God's patience with world conditions. In short, Earth's cup of iniquity will spill over on that day. The first earthquake will not be an ordinary earthquake and it will be distinguished from all previous earthquakes in two ways:

1. This earthquake will be accompanied by manifestations in the heavens and on Earth. There will be rumblings deep in the Earth (which sound like groans and voices), peals of thunder and lightning – these will be simultaneously heard and observed around the world.

2. This earthquake will literally shake all the nations of the world. The Richter scale will not be able to measure the power of this quake.

Then Showers of Meteors Fall

Shortly after the first global earthquake, showers of burning meteors will ignite unquenchable fires around the world. (Revelation 8:7) A meteoric hailstorm is not hard to conceive since scientists have now estimated that more than 2,000 asteroids cross Earth's annual orbit. Many asteroids remain undetected. The likelihood that Earth's gravity will attract some of these asteroids is almost certain. "It is inevitable," scientists say, "Earth will once again be hit by an asteroid large enough to cause mass extinctions . . . ." (*National Geographic*, January 1985, page 47).

Scientists Clark Chapman and David Morrison startled 4,000 geo-scientists at the American Geophysical Union in San Francisco in December 1989, saying, "In terms of risk, the significant danger [from asteroids] comes from impacts with global implications. Statistically, the greatest risk to each of us is [that] . . . the impact could cause a global disruption of crops and/or food distribution systems, leading to widespread starvation and perhaps the death of most of the Earth's human population. We call this a civilization-threatening impact." At the time of the meeting in 1989, Dr. Chapman was a scientist at the Planetary Science Institute in Tucson, Arizona, and Dr. Morrison was chief of the Space Science Division at NASA's Ames Research Center in Mountain View, California.

Scientists have known for years that asteroids and meteorites strike the Earth and moon in predictable patterns. In fact, scientists observed a "near miss" when Asteroid 1989 FC (approximately 1,200 to 2,400 feet in diameter) missed Earth by a margin of only six hours. It was traveling at 46,000 mph. If it had hit Earth, Dr. Bevan French, an expert at NASA's Solar System Exploration Division, calculated it would have released energy equivalent to 20,000 hydrogen bombs. If it had hit a metropolitan area such as Tokyo, Los Angeles or New York, millions of people would have died instantly. Fortunately, most meteorites that have impacted the Earth in recent times have been small and have had no significant consequence. However, news reports of fireballs and meteorites are given regularly. As an example, on November 22, 1996 a "small" meteorite impacted the Earth in Honduras, making a crater 150 feet in diameter.

Science Takes Another Look

Dr. Eugene Shoemaker was one of the first scientists to conclude that Earth had been previously impacted by large asteroids. This idea, widely controversial among geo-scientists in the late 70's, has now become widely accepted due to the mounting evidence which continues to accumulate from research centers around the world. Few scientific skeptics about this subject can be found these days, since the comet Shoemaker-Levy 9 impacted the planet Jupiter's surface in July 1994. One impact site on Jupiter is wide enough to comfortably accommodate two planets the size of Earth. Now, geo-scientists are convinced that our planet has experienced horrific impacts from large asteroids in the past. However, erosion, which constantly changes the face of the Earth, made detection of impact craters difficult. In addition, since 75% of Earth's surface is covered with water, detection of ocean impacts made study almost impossible. Now, with the help of NASA satellites, more and more impact sites have been discovered.

Scientists have identified more than 130 land-craters caused by asteroid or meteorite impacts. The three largest craters are found in Canada, South Africa and off the western coast of Mexico. Each crater has a diameter of about 120 - 150 miles. The largest known crater in the United States is about

18 miles wide and is located in Manson, Iowa. Even though craters are sprinkled over various continents, few are as distinct in appearance as Meteor Crater in Arizona. According to Richard A. F. Grieve, Ph.D., a scientist with the Geological Survey of Canada (*Scientific American*, April 1990), the "tiny" iron meteorite which caused Meteor Crater in Arizona was less than 200 feet in diameter and weighed approximately one million tons. It hit the Earth traveling about 35,000 mph and released energy equivalent to the most powerful nuclear devices available today. Meteor Crater is about two-thirds of a mile wide and 640 feet deep.

The amount of damage caused by an impact is relative to the momentum and the direction of impact. Earth is traveling about 72,000 mph in its annual orbit around the Sun. So, if a meteor traveling at 40,000 mph hits "head on" with Earth, the energy released would be equivalent to a 112,000 mph collision! *National Geographic* magazine featured an impressive article titled "Extinctions" in its June 1989 edition, which reported the findings of scientists studying the effects of ancient asteroid impacts. This article is still timely since the Bible and scientists agree that Earth will be impacted by cosmic debris again.

The *National Geographic* article proposed the following scenario: "Giant meteorite strikes Earth, setting the planet afire. Volcanoes erupt, tsunamis crash into the continents. The sky grows dark for months, perhaps years. Unable to cope with the catastrophic changes in climate, countless species are wiped off the face of the planet" (page 686). The article goes on to suggest that great fires resulting from an asteroid would destroy crops, trees and vegetation. Even worse, wind storms created by the fires would destroy buildings hundreds of miles from the impact. Dust and smoke from the fires would find their way into the jet stream and block much of the sun's light thus altering the world's climate and the chances of human survival!

Will Asteroids Again Impact Earth?

Will our gravitational field attract any of these celestial bodies? "Sooner or later, it is inevitable," scientists say. "Civilization-threatening" asteroids (rocks having a diameter of one to 10 miles) are so tiny in space that scientists rarely detect their presence until they are very close to Earth. Scientists calculate that Asteroid 1989 FC will return and may be even closer to Earth at some point in the near future! This is the meteorite that missed Earth by only six hours in March 1989. What is shocking about Asteroid 1989 FC is that it was not detected until *after* it had passed by Earth.

Does Revelation Predict Asteroid Impacts?

One thing that makes scientific predictions about asteroid impacts interesting is that the *same* conclusions are being reached by people studying the prophecies of Revelation. The Bible also predicts the impact of "civilization-threatening asteroids and meteorites!" Revelation 8:7-11 describes a scenario that closely mirrors the results of what scientists anticipate from such impacts. Revelation symbolizes these events as "trumpets" because trumpets were used in ancient times as a means to arouse people or sound an alarm. Indeed, the seven trumpets of Revelation are harbingers or announcements of the soon appearing of Jesus Christ.

Great Balls of Fire

The first trumpet consists of a large meteoric shower of burning hail. Obviously, many people would die in a catastrophe of this type. Notice what Revelation says, **"The first angel sounded his trumpet, and there came hail and fire mixed with blood, and it was hurled down upon the Earth. A third of the Earth was burned up, a third of the trees were burned up, and all the green grass was burned up."** (Revelation 8:7) John describes great fires caused by burning hail that reduce a third of the Earth, a third of the trees and all the green grass (including crops) to ashes. It is interesting to note that the quantity of one-third is used 12 times throughout the seven trumpets:

1/3 of the Earth will be burned up
1/3 of the trees will be burned up
1/3 of the sea will turn into blood
1/3 of the sea creatures will die
1/3 of the ships on the sea will sink
1/3 of the rivers and springs will become contaminated
1/3 of the light from the sun will be taken away
1/3 of the light from the moon will be taken away
1/3 of the light from the stars will be taken away
1/3 of the day will be without light
1/3 of the night will be without light
1/3 of the troops will be killed in the sixth trumpet war

So, what is the significance of one-third? The answer is generosity, for two-thirds are spared. In ancient times, when a tribe/nation refused to pay tribute to the king controlling the land, it was common practice for the offended king to attack the rebellious city and totally destroy it – men, women and children. However, if the king was in a generous mood, he would often spare one-third of the city's inhabitants from destruction (and thus maintain his tax base). Notice this text: **"David also defeated the Moabites** [who had refused to pay him tribute]. **He made them lie down on the ground and measured them off with a length of cord. Every two lengths of them were put to death, and the third length was allowed to live. So the Moabites became subject to David and brought tribute** [tax]." (2 Samuel 8:2)

The same pattern can be seen in God's dealings with Israel. He tolerated the rebellion of Israel for many years, but when Israel's cup had reached its full measure, God used His servant Nebuchadnezzar (Jeremiah 25:9), and destroyed two-thirds of Israel. Because God is a generous King, He spared one-third (the remnant) by scattering them throughout the world. God told Ezekiel, **"A third of your people will die of the plague or perish by famine inside you; a third will fall by the sword outside your walls; and a third I will scatter to the winds and pursue with drawn sword."** (Ezekiel 5:12)

Again, the balance of mercy can be observed in the days of Zechariah. God said, **"'In the whole land,' declares the Lord, 'two-thirds will be struck down and perish; yet**

one-third will be left in it. This third I will bring into the fire; I will refine them like silver and test them like gold. They will call on my name and I will answer them; I will say, 'They are my people,' and they will say, 'The Lord is our God.'" (Zechariah 13:8,9)

So, the extensive use of one-third within the seven trumpets reveals God's generosity with a rebellious world. The trumpet-judgments are redemptive. If a generous king spared one-third of a rebellious nation in ancient times, what can be said of the King of kings who spares two-thirds of the elements mentioned in the seven trumpets? In fact, if God struck down two-thirds, it is conceivable that all life on this planet could perish in a few weeks!

Many people ask how the destructive thirds described in the trumpets connect with the destruction of one-fourth of the Earth (mentioned in the fourth seal – Revelation 6:7-8). The answer is that when all of the death and destruction caused by the first four trumpets is added together, a fourth of the Earth's population will be dead. (The martyrdom of the fifth seal and the sixth trumpet war is another massive reduction in Earth's population. Also, many of the wicked die during the first five of the seven last plagues. Perhaps the number of people who will be alive when Christ returns will represent about 33% of those who now live on the planet.)

Calamitous Impact on the Sea

Of course, the second trumpet follows the burning meteors of the first trumpet. John describes a great impact upon the sea: **"The second angel sounded his trumpet, and something like a huge mountain, all ablaze, was thrown into the sea. A third of the sea turned into blood, a third of the living creatures in the sea died, and a third of the ships were destroyed."** (Revelation 8:8,9)

This scene apparently describes a large asteroid, the size of a mountain, hitting the sea. The term "mountain" is a very accurate term to describe a large asteroid when you consider that an asteroid, only one mile in diameter, sitting on the surface of the Earth would be a mountain 5,280 feet high! John's description of an asteroid impact on the sea is identical to recent scientific studies. For example, the resulting tidal wave would destroy ships for hundreds of miles in every direction — even those docked in remote seaports. Think about the commotion caused in the ocean after such an impact! (See Luke 21:25.) According to scientists at the University of California, the asteroid would be so hot that it would make a large part of the ocean water anoxic (oxygen deficient) by simply boiling the oxygen out of a large area of the sea. The temperature of the water would also dramatically rise, both from the actual impact as well as from warmer water (heated by volcanic vents) deep within the ocean being forced to the surface. This hot water would kill whatever creature life was left. The warm, anoxic water resulting from the impact would also provide a perfect environment for the growth of red algae or what is known as red tide. John said the sea turned to blood. This appropriately describes the appearance of red algae, which thrives in oxygen deficient water!

Horrific Impact on Land

John describes the third trumpet as a great star that impacts the Earth. **"The third angel sounded his trumpet, and a great star, blazing like a torch, fell from the sky on a third of the rivers and on the springs of water – the name of the star is Wormwood. A third of the waters turned bitter, and many people died from the waters that had become bitter."** (Revelation 8:10,11)

Many prophecy experts insist on a symbolic interpretation of these verses, maintaining that they do not believe these things could literally happen. However, two compelling reasons eliminate the possibility of a symbolic interpretation. First, each event described by John is physically consistent with the literal outcome he gives. Second, if these texts are symbolic, where is the explanation or interpretation of these symbols within the Bible?

Suppose a large star (asteroid or comet), blazing like a torch, were to impact one of Earth's seven continents. What would be the consequence? Ground waves would sheer water wells and sewer lines for hundreds of miles in all directions. Earthquakes and tremors would occur for many days as enormous tectonic forces beneath the surface of the Earth adjust to the impact. Remember, a large asteroid impact would release the energy of thousands of nuclear bombs. The end result is that drinking water would become contaminated by broken sewer systems and toxic waste buried in landfills that leak into subterranean aquifers. Millions of people in large cities would drink the contaminated water, become sick and die. Notice that Revelation 8:10,11 predicts many people will die from drinking bitter water that has become unsafe as a direct consequence of a star hitting the Earth! It is easy to understand why the star is called Wormwood. Wormwood simply means "poisonous." (Jeremiah 9:15 KJV)

Sun, Moon and Stars Darkened

The fourth trumpet follows the first three trumpets and the result is that the sun, moon and stars turn dark. (Revelation 8:12) It is conceivable that the darkness John saw is similar to what occurred in the northwestern part of the United States during the Mount St. Helens eruption in 1980. Although Revelation does not say *why* the sun, moon and stars turn dark, this phenomenon would be consistent with volcanic eruptions. The cumulative effects of a giant earthquake, a meteoric storm of burning hail and two asteroid impacts could certainly disrupt the fragile balance of Earth's tectonic plates. As the tectonic plates strain to readjust, enormous energy would be released. Volcanoes would erupt, belching magma and ash in a series of explosions that would dwarf the blasts of Mount St. Helens and Mount Pinatubo in the Philippines.

The first three trumpets send megatons of dust, soot and debris into the atmosphere. Chains of volcanic eruptions (around the Ring of Fire) belch more dust in the form of volcanic ash, causing extended darkness around the world. Millions of burning acres and resulting windstorms insure that the jet stream is affected. One ounce of soot absorbs

25,000 times the amount of sunlight that one ounce of dust absorbs! Given this physical fact, it is not hard to see how a band of darkness could encircle the middle third of Earth.

Same Conclusions and Some Predictions

What makes the first four trumpets so uncanny is that scientists and Bible students are not only arriving at the same conclusions – that asteroids and meteorites will impact Earth – but they are also surprised by the consistent harmony of results. Will Earth be pummeled by rocks raining from heaven? More and more scientists are convinced it is inevitable, and so are students of Revelation.

In God we Trust?

God knows the end from the beginning. Consequently, 2,000 years ago He had Revelation written in such a way that when the time of the end came, the final generation on Earth could know that it is the last generation. (Amos 3:7) God also gave us His Word that we would have hope, comfort and patience. When God breaks His silence, the world's financial systems will collapse. The wonderful infrastructures we depend on for every aspect of life will be gone. In this coming atmosphere of terror, fear and anxiety, God will open the minds of men and women to see His moment-by-moment interest in them. The human response will be varied. Millions will become despondent and curse God – even to the point of taking their own lives – while others will zealously turn to religion as a means to save themselves. Those who know how to live by faith will trust in God for survival and salvation. They will also be anxious to share with others the purpose of God's visitations.

As we continue to review the end-time story, you will see that Revelation not only predicts asteroid impacts and global darkness, but it also explains man's response to these horrific events. You cannot afford to miss this part of the story. So, stay tuned. You need to know what world leaders are going to do.

Chapter 4

Asteroid Impact Immediately Changes Life

If the explanation of the first four trumpets in the previous chapter seems to be reasonable, and the impact studies done by scientists are within reason, then Revelation provides a very compelling story. The story is not, I repeat, is not disconnected from the international backdrop that exists when the meteors and asteroids collide with our planet. Revelation's story not only predicts the horrific events that immediately change life on Earth, but it also reveals the reactions of religious and political powers at the time the events occur! To understand the actions and reactions of world leaders, consider this simple scenario of Earth's condition after the first four trumpets.

Nature's Dilemma

Scientists predict that wildfires set by a meteor shower could last for months. With megatons of ejecta and ash from the fires circulating in the atmosphere, global darkness would compound a miserable problem. Combine the destruction of meteoric firestorms with two large asteroid impacts and any optimist would seriously doubt the possibility of survival on Earth.

Even if food crops survived the wildfires, few crops would reach maturity because the sun's light would not shine through clouds of ash and soot. This is especially true of food crops, such as corn, which require 100+ days of sunlight to reach maturity. All edible food will be nonexistent. (In 1994, the world's stockpile of food was less than 60 days.) In addition to this, the rain would become so acidic that it would be lethal to plant and animal life, even though it might fall hundreds of miles away from the actual impact site. Earth's delicate ecosphere of life would be damaged beyond repair!

This is why many scientists are now warning that an asteroid could produce a "civilization-threatening impact." Revelation's story also gives clues regarding the numerous physical conditions on Earth during the first four trumpets. For example, Revelation 11:6 indicates that certain places on Earth will go without rain for three years. Also, famine is one of the judgments mentioned in the fourth seal. (Revelation 6:7,8) Further, Revelation 8:11 says that many people will die of drinking contaminated water.

Since medical malpractice litigation has removed or limited the production of many vaccines, there will be great shortages of lifesaving vaccines. Disease will become rampant and every person will question his ability to survive. Jesus said, **"For then there will be great distress, unequaled from the beginning of the world until now – and never to be equaled again. If those days had not been cut short,**

no one would survive, but for the sake of the elect those days will be shortened." (Matthew 24:21,22)

Global Economic Ruin

What will happen to Earth's global economy if the predictions of the scientists and this interpretation of the first four trumpets of Revelation are true?

1. Meteoric showers of burning hail from the first trumpet would ignite great forest fires all over the world. In just a few days a critical natural resource would be destroyed that cannot be replenished in decades. Trees and their by-products are used for the production of paper, building materials and many, many other items. But most of all, trees produce oxygen. If you add millions of acres in wheat, corn and other food crops to the burning inferno, you can see how respiratory problems could kill millions of people and livestock. Mass graves will be everywhere. Food will become as scarce as gold. Never in the history of the world will the index of human suffering reach this level. (Matthew 24:21,22)

2. If an asteroid, one mile in diameter, hits an ocean, it would create tidal waves exceeding 3,000 feet in height. Thousands, perhaps millions of people would drown. The Bible says that one-third of the ships would sink as a result of a tidal wave produced by this impact. Super-tankers carrying millions of barrels of oil would be spilled into the ocean. Cargo from Japan, Russia, China, America and other countries, worth billions of dollars,

would rest on the bottom of the ocean. Great coastal cities, as well as much of the coastline would be destroyed. Entire islands would be washed away! Countries that heavily depend on oil and food supplies arriving by sea will experience immediate shortages of all kinds. Even worse, many countries depend on their fertile coast lands for valuable food crops. The destruction of these areas would bring dire circumstances to every human being, especially when you consider that many people keep less than one week's food supply on hand. Large insurance companies, along with other corporations, would go bankrupt leaving the world's stock markets in total chaos. The domino effect on the economy of all nations would be beyond calculation. Perhaps this kind of speculation sounds like a fairy tale, but Luke talks about the fury of the ocean before Jesus returns by writing, **"There will be signs in the sun, moon and stars. On the Earth, nations will be in anguish and perplexity at the roaring and tossing of the sea. Men will faint from terror, apprehensive of what is coming on the world . . . ."** (Luke 21:25,26)

3. Compound the destruction of our nation's food basket with the horror of contaminated drinking water everywhere, and the situation will grow so desperate that a person would wonder if life could go on at all. Desperate circumstances call for extreme efforts. To stabilize the situation, governments will respond quickly. First, they will, out of necessity, enact contingency or emergency constitutions. This means that martial law will be

implemented to prevent anarchy and the total break-down of government. Stringent laws will be implemented and people will have no choice but to comply. Individual rights will be canceled. The cost of sin is always great – even upon the innocent.

4. To prevent total anarchy, rationing will be implemented. People, full of fear, will do everything they can to obtain food and medicine. Buying and selling of all commodities will be controlled. This will be necessary because every survivor needs a basic number of items to sustain life itself. Who will argue with the drastic economic methods enacted if it means survival? As days turn into weeks and weeks into months, people will give in to despair. Hope for recovery will dim. On every point of the compass there will be destruction and suffering beyond description. All the people of Earth will be in a state of shock. The living will envy the dead.

The Most Important Question

The results that follow the first four trumpets are as dramatic as the devastation caused by those events! In a sentence, the administration of life on planet Earth as we now know it will be changed overnight. Pandemonium, confusion, fear, depression, stupor and distress will rule the day. Out of the depth of human suffering, people will question: "Why did God allow this? Why did He do this? What does He want?"

A great change will occur overnight in the way people think about God. Most Christians talk about God's love, His great salvation and forgiveness, but little is said about the things that make Him angry. Many Christians even deny that God has wrath! Consequently, when His judgments begin to fall, many Christians will be at a loss to reconcile these "Acts of God" with their assumed knowledge of God. Their "faith" will suffer a complete meltdown and fear will overwhelm them.

It is not difficult for God to frighten people. He only needs to tamper with things that make us feel secure to get our attention. When lives and property are destroyed, survivors tend to renew their acquaintance with God. (Have you noticed?) Like Israel of old, all nations will tremble with fear before Almighty God during the days of His visitation. (Exodus 20:18-21) The solution to pleasing or appeasing God – so that His destruction of Earth will stop – will appear simple on the surface. Religious leaders will cry out, "Submit to the authority of God." But how does a person worship the God of Heaven so that His wrath is satisfied?

Religious Revolution

Clergy from all religious systems will come forward with a straightforward explanation of God's judgments. They will quickly adjust their current interpretations to fit the *new* situation. (Perhaps we should ask why they did not proclaim these things *before* they happened since they claim to understand the Bible?) They will say, "These 'Acts of God' have come because we have forgotten our Creator." All around the world, clerics from all faiths will agree saying, "We must repent of our great sins and appease God or we will be totally destroyed."

Jewish, Catholic and Protestant leaders will turn to the Old Testament to prove their point. There is abundant Scriptural support that God sends judgments upon people when they become evil. Some of the Old Testament chapters they may quote are Daniel 9; Isaiah 24, 25; Ezekiel 7; and Jeremiah 25.

As people begin to link the devastations caused by the four trumpets to the idea that God is displeased with the human race, one question will be on everyone's mind: "What must we do to appease God?" Even though different solutions will be offered in different lands, a common theme will develop around the world. Revelation indicates there will be a global rush to appease God and a remarkable surge of worldwide repentance. Currently in the United States, only 39% of the people attend church regularly. This percentage will double overnight! Religion will become a priority and religious leaders with evangelical fervor will lead all nations – almost overnight – into a religious revolution.

Number One Question

The religious revolution will immediately highlight a significant question. There are several different religious systems on Earth and each group worships its God in a different way. Is there *one* right way to worship God? Moslems believe that God is pleased when people obey the teachings of Mohammed. Catholics believe that God is pleased when people obey the pope and the laws of the church. Protestants, Jews, Hindus and other groups have different ideas about what pleases God. Which religious system is right? Does God really care about the way we worship Him? Soon, the issues surrounding this question will become the primary focus for Earth's inhabitants. In today's context, the question appears to be rhetorical, but when billions of people feel God's anger, this question will be foremost in their minds.

Desperate circumstances quickly unite people as they focus on a common problem or solution. (The war between Iraq and the United Nations' coalition of 29 nations led by the United States in 1990 demonstrates this point.) Shortly after the trumpets begin, Revelation predicts the world will participate in the rapid development of a global religious coalition. Instead of a nation's citizens fighting and quarreling among themselves over things like power, land or money, the judgments of God will propel religious leaders into a significant leadership role. Overwhelming devastation will leave people in a state of confused shock. Prompted by terror, controlled by fear and trying to be significant, clerics will call for drastic measures to appease God so His judgments will cease. Since the destruction caused by the first four trumpets is global, the religious leaders will appear to globally unite.

Laws Enforcing Worship

As terror crescendos throughout the world in response to the devastation of the trumpets, governments will pass laws requiring citizens to worship God. Laws will be implemented in every land that demand we respect the laws of God or perish. However, there will be no global consistency in these religious laws; instead, there will be great confusion. Catholics and Protestants will seek laws that agree with their theology, Jews will make laws agreeing with their doctrine, Moslems will want laws respecting their beliefs in Allah, and other groups will demand similar laws. Notice the problem that occurs with diverse religions. How can diverse religions appease one God? Is He a God of many religions?

One World – One God – Many Religions

One organization on Earth stands head and shoulders above all others in terms of diplomatic ties with religious and political leaders all over the world. It is the papacy. The Roman Catholic Church has steadily secured diplomatic connections with almost every segment of Earth's population since John Paul II became Pope in 1978. Currently, the church has formal relations with 163 nations!

When the trumpets begin, the Pope will move quickly to convene a "World Congress" of religious and political bodies. This congress will form a powerful organization that is called "Babylon" in Revelation. (Revelation 13, 17, 18) Perhaps the United Nations will facilitate this organization, I do not know. But understand, the glue that will bond the leaders of the world together will not be politics. It will be immediate concerns about God and His anger. Religious differences will be hastily compromised and efforts to appease God will begin on a global scale. Yet, a global solution will remain elusive. The problem is this: "How does God want all of the Earth to worship Him?" Moslems, Jews, Catholics, Hindus, Protestants and other religious organizations will have fundamentally different answers. But how can one man prove the superiority of his religion over that of another? Thus, the reign of confusion exists for a season. But, when the devil himself appears on Earth during the fifth trumpet, claiming to be God, it will appear that he has the solution for Earth's dilemma. The devil will oppose the solutions of man and will exalt himself above all religions of the world. He will declare that the only way to unite the world into one religion is by dissolving all religions into one. Of course, the world's religious leaders will have to go along! They will "think" he is God!

To address this global diversity, Revelation predicts a global coalition of religious representatives will quickly form. (Revelation 13:1-5) This coalition of religious representatives (seven heads) will join with political leaders (ten horns) to resolve problems resulting from diverse views about God. The name "Babylon" is an appropriate representation of this coalition because "Babylon" refers to a state of gross confusion. (Genesis 11:9) If you compare Daniel 3 with Revelation 13, you will discover that modern Babylon's story parallels the experience of ancient Babylon. Modern Babylon, like ancient Babylon, will be made up of many religions, cultures and nationalities.

What Does God Want?

Revelation 14 explains what God wants. John saw a message going throughout the world saying, **"Fear God and** give him glory, because the hour of his judgment has come. Worship him who made the heavens, the Earth, the sea and the springs of water." (Revelation 14:7) Notice that the last sentence of this verse itemizes the four things afflicted by the first four trumpets! Religious people, the world over, will quickly agree *why* the judgments are falling and *what* they are, but the problem is *how* to implement a global solution that will appease God. What a nightmare! Imagine the chaos of trying to unite different religions on the Earth when each one claims they have the truth and practice the *only* right way to worship God.

Consider the Question

Think about this for a moment. Sincere people all over the Earth worship God according to what they believe to be true worship, and the Bible says that God accepts such worship. According to Romans 2, John 4 and Acts 10:35, God accepts the worship of all people on Earth if they worship Him in spirit and in truth. This means that if anyone worships God with a humble and obedient spirit according to all the truth they know, then God, ever generous and merciful, accepts their worship as genuine.

The human race, however, is not living up to the spirit and truth of what we know to be right! Legislators should realize by now that *laws do not make people good*. Rather, good laws direct good people. Laws also insure that justice and punishment is administered fairly. Laws are only useful if people live by them. But, when the Holy Spirit's promptings are rejected and personal decency and integrity fade within the majority of people, then evil, violence and suffering escalate. Nothing rouses the anger of God more than sexual immorality and violence, because these evil cancers affect the quality of life for generations. History is full of sad examples. Destructive behavior and decadence overtake a nation whenever its people forget their individual accountability to their Creator. This is why, at various times and in different ways, whenever sin fills the cup, God breaks His silence. (Proverbs 6:16-19)

The Gospel Truth

So, an interesting paradox will develop. Lawless behavior is currently everywhere. Political leaders recognize that government structures can only remain intact if there is law and order. The Bible states that when world leaders begin pleading for world order, world peace and safety, God will break His silence. This day must be near because 1 Thessalonians 5:3 says: **"While people are saying, 'Peace and safety,' destruction will come on them suddenly, as labor pains on a pregnant woman, and they will not escape."**

Remember, God has not designed the seven trumpets of Revelation to destroy the world completely. This is why John repetitively uses the "one-third" portion to explain how the elements are harmed. The first four trumpets are used to literally arrest the attention of 6 billion people, so that all will listen to the gospel and learn what God wants. In other words, the world must hear the unvarnished truth about God and His claims upon man. What is the acceptable way to worship Almighty God? Everyone has to know the truth on this matter. This is why Jesus said the gospel must go to every nation and to every person before the end comes. (Matthew 24:14) To accomplish this task, God will empower 144,000 people to proclaim the everlasting gospel. These individuals will explain the appropriate way to glorify God and they will show how it is an integral part of the everlasting gospel. The message of the 144,000 will be in direct opposition to what the religious leaders of Babylon want to do.

The eternal gospel reveals what God wants of us and one of the primary elements of the gospel is worship. Questions regarding worship will cause an enormous controversy which will soon engulf every person on Earth. Each of the world's religious systems claim to have the truth about God and in an effort to please God, each political body will enact laws respecting the prevailing religious belief of its people. Moslems in Iran will enact compulsory laws to reverence Allah on Friday. Catholics and Protestants will enact Sunday laws – claiming that God requires worship on Sunday. Jews and other religious groups will also enact laws regarding respect for God in their lands on certain days. The problem, according to Revelation, is that these coming laws will be contrary to the law of God – which is the legal basis for His wrath in the first place!

God does not accept the worship of human beings if they knowingly reject His commands. This issue will fuel an enormous controversy among the people of Earth at a time when the religious and political leaders of the world are desperately trying to appease God. Revelation predicts that Babylon will enact laws regarding worship, and most of the world will submit to man-made laws rather than obey the law of God. John wrote, **"All inhabitants of the Earth will worship the beast** [Babylon] **– all whose names have not been written in the book of life belonging to the Lamb that was slain from the creation of the world."** (Revelation 13:8)

Chapter 5
Satan Appears in Person

The first four trumpets will reduce life on Earth to complete chaos. Then, the next event described in Revelation is the fifth trumpet. (Revelation 9:1-12) The fifth trumpet reveals that the devil himself, that ancient serpent who spoke to Eve, will physically appear on Earth after the "dust settles" from the asteroid impacts. He may first appear in the Middle East, perhaps Jerusalem. The Bible does not designate a specific location, but many orthodox Jews anticipate the imminent arrival of Messiah to deliver them from their enemies. Their hopes for the coming Messiah would provide an inviting platform for Satan to use to his advantage, especially since many Christians believe the Jews are still God's chosen people. In addition to the Jews' expectation of the coming Messiah, the Arabs also believe a Deliverer will soon appear. So, it is not hard to speculate why the Middle East could be an excellent geographical target for Satan!

When Satan first appears, he will resemble a glorious being and claim to be the "Savior of the World." At that moment in time, the world will be in a very vulnerable position. The cry for help will be everywhere and the enemy of mankind will demonstrate great sympathy for human suffering. To make his deception even more secure, he will perform great and wonderful miracles of blessing. (1 Thessalonians 2:9)

Who is the Devil?

According to the Bible, the devil once had an exalted name. His name was Lucifer – which means "light bearer." A quick review of Isaiah 14:12-17 and Ezekiel 28:12-18 reveals that Lucifer was once a mighty angel in Heaven. Apparently, he became proud, vain and ultimately dissatisfied with the way God was running the universe. Lucifer sowed his seeds of disaffection among the angels which led to a great rebellion in Heaven. According to Revelation 12, Satan and his angels were cast out of Heaven. Jesus told His disciples, **"I saw Satan fall like lightning from heaven."** (Luke 10:18)

Angry and bitter with his defeat, Lucifer focused his hostility toward the ruination of God's special handiwork – planet Earth. He went to the Garden of Eden and led Adam and Eve to disobey God. The devil did not stop with our first parents. Cain, the firstborn of Adam and Eve, became a murderer. As time went by, Earth became so defiled by sin as a result of Satan's influence, that God was grieved that He had even made man! (Genesis 6) Consequently, God washed the Earth clean of sin with a flood of water, sparing just eight people – Noah and his family. Unfortunately, the flood only slowed the devil down for a season. Peter tells us the devil is still alive and goes about seeking whom he may devour! (1 Peter 5:8,9)

Satan Allowed to Live

So, why did God allow the devil to live? Why not extermi-
nate Satan and his angels and spare Earth all the grief? The
answer is both simple and profound.

1. If God had immediately zapped Lucifer and the angels
   who disagreed with Him, what kind of God would He
   be? Based on the evidence, He would have been considered a dictator – a selfish and self-promoting God!
   Think about it, if God quickly exterminates everyone
   who disagrees with Him, He would be the biggest bully
   in the universe. Wouldn't He?

2. God, having infinite wisdom, knows that sin should be
   allowed a brief period of existence (speaking in terms
   of eternity) so all His universe can see the consequences
   of sin. By allowing rebellion to exist for a time, all of
   God's creation (including Satan and his angels) can see
   that God's principles of government are best – not because God says His ways are best – but rather, because
   they have been demonstrated to be righteous.

3. God freely gives the power of choice to each created
   being. His subjects do not have to obey Him, love Him
   or respond to His goodness or generosity. Lucifer and
   his angels have proven this. They have lived long enough
   to demonstrate the consequences of their own choosing. Adam and Eve also demonstrated that they had
   power of choice to disobey God and their choice has
   revealed the dire consequences of sin. Time has vali-

dated that there is no quality of life in rebellion against the ways of God. True, sin may seem to offer pleasure and excitement for a *short* season, but it extracts a far greater price than the value of a cheap thrill. Sin takes us farther than we want to go, and sin costs us more than we want to pay. No matter how well Satan disguises sin, **"the wages of sin is death."** (Romans 6:23)

4. God foreknew the consequences of allowing Satan and his angels to live. Yet, at great expense to Himself, God provided a plan to save all the people who would ever live on Earth. He loved the people of the world so much that He gave us His only Son's life. Jesus was willing to come and die for man so the penalty for sin could be paid! God Himself has paid a much greater price for the existence of sin than any human being will ever know!

So, the conflict between Jesus and Lucifer has been in progress on Earth for nearly 6,000 years. Today, both still strive to win the affections of people. I anticipate this struggle will come to a climax before this decade ends.

Out of the Bottomless Pit

Revelation says the devil is going to enter the realm of our senses and physically appear before our eyes. This process is predicted in Revelation 9 where the devil is portrayed as coming out of the abyss or bottomless pit! To appreciate the prediction and the meaning of John's language, we need to understand a little about ancient history.

People living during Bible times thought the Earth was flat, much like a large plate or basin. Having limited knowledge about the law of gravity, they reasoned that the Earth must be basin-like. They believed the ocean would "drain away" if the world was spherical. So, they believed a bottomless pit would be created if a person dug a hole all the way through the basin of the Earth. Without a bottom, a person could fall into the pit and never be seen again. Understanding John's mind set helps us understand the Biblical term "bottomless pit" or "abyss."

The transliteration of the Greek word *abussos* in English is "abyss." Whether it is called "bottomless pit" or "abyss," the idea is identical. To the ancients, the "bottomless pit" represented the source or origin of evil things. They also believed that demons lived "under the Earth" and they came out of caves or holes which had no bottom or end to them. The term "abyss" or "bottomless pit" is used several times in Revelation. When God revealed last-day events to John in A.D. 95, God used imagery that John was familiar with. John saw the devil and his angels ascend out of a bottomless pit and John refers to this event in several places in Revelation. Many people are surprised to learn that Revelation predicts the physical appearance of Satan on Earth for a period of time just before the coming of Jesus! Revelation not only tells us when, but also tells us why!

The Fifth Trumpet

God only allows the devil to physically appear *after* a significant part of the world has heard the gospel. By the time

Satan appears, most of Earth has already heard and rejected the gospel the 144,000 have proclaimed. Therefore, God releases and empowers the devil to rule over those who refused to recognize Him as the Almighty. This is an interesting point about the Great Tribulation: Each person will have a master, either by choice or by force. Who will it be? The time periods in Revelation suggest that the devil will appear about two years after the fourth trumpet sounds.

When the fifth trumpet of Revelation 9:1-11 begins and the bottomless pit is "unlocked," God shows John something that looks like a great swarm of locusts coming up out of the Earth. As the swarm draws closer to him, John can see that they look like riders on horses. Directing the riders is an angel king whose name in Hebrew is Abaddon and in Greek, is Apollyon. Both names mean the same thing – "destroyer." The language of Revelation 9:1-11 is parallel to Joel 2:1-11. Joel describes the coming of the Lord with His mighty host of angels. Joel also describes the scene as a great swarm of horses prepared for battle. In Revelation, John uses the same language as Joel to describe what he sees, except the swarm emanates from the bottomless pit.

The release of Satan and his angels from the bottomless pit reveals three important things. First, Satan will NOT come in the clouds of glory *exactly* like Jesus. Although Satan will do everything in his power to imitate Jesus' second coming, God limits the devil's deception. Satan will appear to come down from the clouds in various places. This is why Jesus said, **"At that time if anyone says to you, 'Look,**

here is the Christ!' or, 'There he is!' do not believe it."
(Matthew 24:23) Second, God will not allow Satan to physically appear on Earth until the first four trumpets have
sounded. Last, God has designed that the physical appearing of the devil will force everyone into a firm decision.
Salvation is still possible for anyone who will repent of their
rebellion and turn to God before the seventh trumpet sounds.

According to Revelation 9:3-6, after Satan and his evil angels appear, they have five months to torment "unsaved"
people. Just what the torment is and how it is inflicted, is
not clear from Scripture. However, what we do know is that
the torment will hurt like a scorpion's sting. The people who
are afflicted will long to die, but they will actually survive
the ordeal. The point of allowing the devil to afflict "unsaved" people is found in this: God's offer of salvation is
still open when Satan appears. In other words, anyone harmed
by the devil can be delivered from agony if he will turn
from evil and submit to the Lord. (See Numbers 21:6-9.)

An Angel of Light

When Satan appears, his radiant countenance will so dazzle
the people of Earth that many will believe his claims that he
is God based on his appearance alone. Paul says, "**. . . for
Satan himself masquerades as an angel of light.**" (2 Corinthians 11:14) Revelation states that when Satan appears, he
will be so dazzling and glorious that most people will be
awestruck when they actually see him! "**. . . The inhabitants of the Earth whose names have not been written in
the book of life from the creation of the world will be**

astonished **when they see the beast . . . ."** (Revelation 17:8, Italics added.)

Satan Works Miracles, Signs and Wonders

Satan's first work after appearing "in the flesh" as a glorious God-man will be to convince the world that he is divine – that he is actually God. Paul warns, **"Don't let anyone deceive you in any way, for that day (the second coming) will not come until the rebellion occurs and the man of lawlessness is revealed, the man doomed to destruction. He opposes and exalts himself over everything that is called God or is worshiped, and even sets himself up in God's temple, proclaiming himself to be God . . . The coming of the lawless one will be in accordance with the work of Satan displayed in all kinds of counterfeit miracles, signs and wonders, and in every sort of evil that deceives those who are perishing. They perish because they refused to love the truth and so be saved."** (2 Thessalonians 2:3,4,9,10)

Calls Fire Down Out of Heaven

The one miracle that Satan will use above all others to convince people that he is God will be to call fire down out of heaven at will! This "proof of divinity" will make his deceptions secure for many, many people. John says, **"And he performed great and miraculous signs, even causing fire to come down from heaven to Earth in full view of men. Because of the signs he was given power to do on behalf of the first beast, he deceived the inhabitants of the Earth . . . ."** (Revelation 13:13,14)

John also describes the appearing of Satan as a "lamb-like" beast. (Revelation 13:11) The intended contrast is obvious – Revelation refers to Jesus as "The Lamb" more than 29 times. John describes Satan as a "lamb-like" beast, because the devil masquerades as Jesus. John also warns that Satan will make every effort to deceive the world.

The Scene Reviewed

Satan's appearance will be the grandest deception ever to occur on Earth and to comprehend the consequences, we need to review the situation existing at that time. When Satan appears, every quadrant of Earth will have experienced massive destruction and suffering as a result of the first four trumpets. Earth's skies will have been dark for a time, and billions of people (that's billions) will have grown hopeless. The death toll will be numberless, and tens of thousands of people will continue to die every day from famine and disease. People will be filled with despair, and clerics will continue to lament that people must repent and worship God so His anger will subside. Religious persecution and intolerance will be everywhere because Babylon (the one world order) will be determined to settle the issue. Foremost in all people's minds at that time will be the question, "What must we do to appease God so that He will stop the suffering?"

Into this nightmare the devil gloriously appears. Satan uses incredible displays of signs and wonders to deceive, if possible, the very elect. (Matthew 24:24-25) His purpose has always been to destroy this world and when his day of opportunity comes, it will be a splendid moment for him to fulfill this ambition. The devil cleverly turns the majority of the world away from hearing and believing the gospel, and in time, will force the world's people into false worship on pain of death! Revelation 13:15 says, **"He, [Satan] . . . caused all who refused to worship the image to be killed."**

Worship the Image or Die

What is the image of the beast? If the beast of Revelation 13:1-8 represents the seven religious and ten political entities of the world, then the image is the consolidation of the world's religions into one global church/state. (Nebuchadnezzar created a replica of the *image* he saw in his dream as recorded in Daniel 2 by consolidating the diverse metals of the human figure into one metal: Gold.) When Catholics, Jews, Protestants, Moslems and Hindus believe that Satan is actually God, they will be willing to do whatever he demands. He will demand that all religions be dissolved into one religion. This will require everyone to leave his church behind. The new church or "image" will be the devil's church and all who join it will receive the necessities of life (food, medicine, etc.). To be sure only "members" receive these items, each person must receive a mark or tattoo showing that they belong to the "image" church.

A Day of Testing

The seven trumpets are specifically designed to awaken the world to the return of Jesus Christ. If anyone wishes to receive salvation during this time-period, he or she must worship the Creator of the heavens, Earth, the sea and springs of water. (Revelation 14:6-7) The word worship simply means "to render obedience." Every Christian should know that man *is not saved* by obedience, for the Bible states that we are saved by faith. (Ephesians 2:8,9) So, the primary purpose of the Great Tribulation is to test our faith by challenging our loyalty. God will test the faith of all men and women by administering a life or death test of loyalty. In this context, each person's faith will be revealed – whom will they obey? People choosing to submit to the laws of man or the devil – will reject God's sovereign authority. Others choosing to submit to the laws of God – will reject man's authority dictating how or when God is to be worshiped. It is interesting that the penalty for rejecting either God's laws or man's laws will be death. (Daniel 3 and Daniel 6 contain two stories that demonstrate the ultimate test of faith.)

The irony in this story is very evident: The 144,000 will proclaim that all must obey God's law and at the same time Babylon is *demanding the same thing!* Remember, clerics from all religious systems throughout the world will be proclaiming with a united voice, "God has caused these judgments on Earth because we are sinful." They will also say that God must be appeased before His judgments will cease and if the people of Earth do not respond soon, God will ultimately destroy everyone. As a result, the religious leaders of Babylon will demand that laws be enforced requiring obedience to God. Moslems will appeal to the Koran for authority about the worship of God; Jews will appeal to the Talmud, the Mishna and the Torah; and Catholics will look to the Pope and the catechism for directions on worship. To what authority will Protestants appeal – the Bible?

A Holy Day Mystery

God has clearly expressed how His subjects are to worship Him. This is not a matter left to human design. Unfortunately, during the past 6,000 years, the devil has obscured God's truth and implemented many false religions around the world. During the end-time, Babylon (Satan's union of world religions) will face a peculiar problem. Each religious system demands the worship of *one* God in different ways! For example, Moslems regard Friday, the Jews regard Saturday, and Christians regard Sunday as a holy day! Remember, Revelation 13:8 says, **"All inhabitants of the Earth will worship the beast [Babylon, which has seven heads and ten horns] – all whose names have not been written in the book of life belonging to the Lamb that was slain . . . ."** Is there a right way and a wrong way to worship God? Is God specific about how we must worship Him? Yes.

The story of Cain and Abel illustrates the primary difference between true and false worship. Both men worshiped. Both brothers built altars. Abel worshiped God by obediently sacrificing a lamb according to God's instruction. Cain did as *he* thought best. In effect, Cain *presumed* to tell his Creator how He would be worshiped. Thus, Cain exalted himself above God and God refused to recognize his offering. (Genesis 4:1-16)

As a result of rejection, Cain became violently angry and killed his brother. Why? John warns, **"Do not be like Cain,** who belonged to the evil one and murdered his brother. And why did he murder him? Because his own actions were evil and his brother's were righteous. Do not be surprised, my brothers, if the world hates you." (1 John 3:12,13) John says Cain's "act of worship" was evil! In fact, it was blasphemous, because Cain took the prerogative of God. *He thought he could tell God how He should be worshiped!* Think about this. If a created being can tell his Creator how or when He is to be worshiped, then the created being has usurped authority over the Creator. How can a human being presume such a thing?

The crux of the matter is this. God accepts our worship if we worship Him in spirit and truth; that is, if we worship God according to all we know to be true. The eternal gospel that goes to every nation, kindred, tongue and people contains information about the worship of God that will be *new* to most people. The first angel's message says loudly, **"Fear God . . . and worship the Creator."** (Revelation 14:7) The reason the first angel's message begins in this manner is because most of the world neither fears God nor worships Him correctly! God knows our spiritual darkness and He has winked at our ignorance, but this is about to change. When God sends the glorious light of the everlasting gospel throughout the world, He will expel the darkness Satan has placed around the subject of God's authority and worship. The honest in heart will receive the first angel's message and worship God according to the truth found in the everlasting gospel.

Worship the Creator

How are human beings to worship God? As written earlier, God has not left the worship of our Creator to human design. God clearly explains in the Ten Commandments how He is to be worshiped. Carefully review the first four commandments. They are found in Exodus 20:3-11:

1. **"You shall have no other gods before [other than] me."**

2. **"You shall not make for yourself an idol in the form of anything in heaven above or on the Earth beneath or in the waters below. You shall not bow down to them or worship them; for I, the Lord your God, am a jealous God, punishing the children for the sin of the fathers to the third and fourth generation of those who hate me, but showing love to thousands who love me and keep my commandments."**

3. **"You shall not misuse the name of the Lord your God, for the Lord will not hold anyone guiltless who misuses his name."**

4. **"Remember the Sabbath day by keeping it holy. Six days you shall labor and do all your work, but the seventh day is a Sabbath to the Lord your God. On it you shall not do any work, neither you, nor your son or daughter, nor your manservant or maidservant, nor your animals, nor the alien within your gates. For in six days the Lord made the heavens and the Earth, the sea, and all that is in them, but he**

rested on the seventh day. Therefore the Lord blessed the Sabbath day and made it holy."

These commandments outline the basics of true worship. They explain the reverence and respect due our Creator. We are not to obey or reverence any other God. We are not to create an idol and bow down before it. We are not to use or represent the name of God in a careless way. And we are to keep the seventh day of the week holy as a memorial to our Creator and His creation of Earth by not working on that day (the Sabbath).

The Ten Commandments are divided into two groups. The first four commandments deal with man's relationship to God, and the last six deal with man's relationship to his neighbor. Actually, the Ten Commandments summarize the two essential laws of life. Jesus said, **". . .'Love the Lord your God with all your heart and with all your soul and with all your mind.' This is the first and greatest commandment. And the second is like it: 'Love your neighbor as yourself.' All the Law and the Prophets hang on these two commandments."** (Matthew 22:37-40; Jesus quotes from Deuteronomy 6:5; Leviticus 19:18.)

Love is the basis of salvation. Love makes submission a joy. If love is the foundation of a relationship, it is genuine. The two commandments that Jesus mentioned are defined in the Ten Commandments. The meaning of love is not left to human definition. Unfortunately, the word "love" today commonly means sex, lust or passion. What a perversion! Jesus came from Heaven to correct human misunderstanding on this point. According to Jesus, true love is a high and holy principle that produces joyful obedience! **"Whoever has my commands and obeys them, he is the one who loves me. He who loves me will be loved by my Father, and I too will love him and show myself to him . . . If anyone loves me, he will obey my teaching . . . He who does not love me will not obey my teaching . . . ."** (John 14:21-24)

As you would expect, Satan has veiled the importance of the first four commandments from most of the world. He has specifically hidden the requirements of the fourth commandment which contains divine instruction on the time of worship. Satan's purpose for doing this is quite simple. God created a basic, innate desire within man to worship Him. Man needs something to look up to – something to worship. Unfortunately, most of us, do not realize our accountability to our Creator and when man forgets his Creator, he soon creates his own god(s).

Satan has enjoyed enormous success in displacing the Creator with man-made gods. God requires one-seventh of our time and one-tenth of our money. Many have no idea of God's claims upon us. But, everyone has a God and we only need to discover where each person spends their time and money to discover his or her god(s).

God will use the trumpets to strip away our false sense of security and our foolish attraction for gods of wood, metal and stone. God will awaken people all over the world to see their rebellious attitude against Him. The knowledge of the true, living and omnipotent God will break out all over the

Earth! God's silence will be shattered and all creation will know that He sits enthroned in Heaven. He is Almighty – He is Sovereign. The everlasting gospel will contain a clarion call to worship the Creator on His holy day – Saturday, the seventh day of the week.

Review the fourth commandment on page 100 and notice the following:

1. The seventh day of the week was declared holy because God rested on the seventh day to commemorate the creation of the world! The word *holy* simply means "set apart." God made the seventh day uniquely different from the other six days at creation! He set the seventh day apart from the others. (Genesis 2:2,3) This is no different than marriage. When a man and woman are married, they are set apart from all others by vows of fidelity.

2. Knowing that Satan would lead the world to forget or deny the holiness of the seventh day Sabbath, God begins the fourth commandment with "Remember." (Exodus 20:8)

3. Contrary to what many say, the seventh day *alone* is holy. The other six days, according to God, are for our use and work. (Exodus 20:9)

Were the Ten Commandments Abolished?

If you ask most Christians about the Ten Commandments, they will agree that nine of the ten are valid and important.

They will agree that it is morally wrong to steal, kill, commit adultery, curse God or worship idols. In fact, most of the world intellectually agrees with nine of the Ten Commandments and readily acknowledges that they are essential within a moral society. But if you ask about the fourth commandment, you will suddenly hear that the Ten Commandments were nailed to the cross and are no longer binding.

For centuries Protestant and Catholic clerics have taught that the Ten Commandments *are not* binding. Therefore, most laymen see no reason to be concerned about the contents of the fourth commandment. If we reason from cause to effect, we would recognize the hopeless state in which our society finds itself today is due to lawlessness. Parents have not taught their children the importance of God's law. When the training of moral law is neglected in childhood, moral order eventually becomes nonexistent and another law, the law of the jungle, prevails. In the jungle, the strongest rule by evil whim (i.e., machine gun, brute force). When God's laws are made void, safety, virtue and morality flee. The result is chaos, suffering, sexual depravity beyond description and needless death. If the understanding of moral law does not exist within the heart, then decadence, chaos and misery overtake society. This is the great tragedy of this century. Unfortunately, parents have left a legacy of degenerate conduct that affects global society.

Law and Grace

Many Christians refuse to consider the close harmony that exists between law and grace, even though they apply these concepts in their lives every day. Law and grace are brother and sister – they are inseparably related. In fact, they cannot exist without each other. We need grace *because* there is law. If God had no law, grace would not be necessary! Paul and John say that when there is no law, there is no sin! (See Romans 4:15 and 1 John 3:4-6.) However, grace does not lessen the obedience that laws require either! (Romans 3:31)

If a judge pardons a speeding ticket, does this act of "grace" release the offender from the requirement to obey the speed limit in the future? Not at all. The law remains intact and grace offers the offender another chance. In practice, the harmony between law and grace is easy to understand. For example, when two people are united in love, there are certain nonnegotiable rules the couple must follow if they are to maintain fidelity to the relationship. Faithfulness is one nonnegotiable rule. So it is with our Creator. If we love Him, we must abide by His nonnegotiable rules, not for salvation, but to maintain a relationship. A person cannot have a relationship with God without obeying Him. God is not our equal. He is Sovereign God of the Universe. The Bible says, **"When Abram was ninety-nine years old, the Lord appeared to him and said, 'I am God Almighty; walk before me and be blameless.' "** (Genesis 17:1) Abram, as well as Enoch and Noah, all walked before God and were blameless, not because of their actions, but because they loved God. (Genesis 5:24; 6:9)

God's nonnegotiable rules for man are His Ten Commandments and Christians are often confused by the relationship between man and God's law. Remember that obeying God's laws have never brought salvation, for *salvation is not based on obedience.* Salvation is based on our "willingness," our attitude toward obedience. Obeying God's laws are singularly for our benefit – not His. This is why disobeying God's laws always brings suffering and death. If we live in harmony with God's laws, we can live life to the fullest, as God created life to be lived. If we ignore God's laws, death and misery are the end results. If we live by God's laws, we can enjoy the pursuit of happiness and the fullness of life that He wants us to have. If we ignore them, the consequences are self-evident, even more, the newspapers print the horrible results daily.

Categories of People

People may be grouped into various categories according to their views on the authority of the Ten Commandments.

a. Some people are simply ignorant about the requirements of God's law. These people have not had sufficient reason or opportunity to know and inquire about God's authority or will.

b. Some people are negligent or careless about God's law. These people know about God's law, but they confuse common things with sacred things. Their pursuit of Earthly things takes a high priority, with religious matters eventually becoming a low priority.

c. Some people observe law as a ritual necessary for salvation. These people think they keep the law and feel justified by their assumed righteousness. Being technically right on a few points is very important to them.

d.   Some people deny implicit law. These people reject the idea that the Ten Commandments are necessary or binding today. Many Christians believe this without realizing the awful consequences of their position. When pressed on this matter, most Christians will admit that a violation of any of the remaining nine of the Ten Commandments is sin.

e.   Some people openly and defiantly rebel against God's law. They do not want to know God, nor do they care what He says.

f.   Some people honestly seek to know God and sincerely want to live in harmony with the principles of God's law. These people are willing to go where God sends, to be all that He wants, and to do all that He asks.

This last group lives by faith. They realize that the law of God is based on two great principles: love to God and love to man. To obey the first four commandments reveals our love for God and to obey the last six reveals our love for man. To obey the commandments of Jesus *out of gratitude and love* is to know His salvation.

There is a two-step process which helps to harmonize our life with the law of God. First, realize that no one can be saved through obeying the law. The human nature is inherently attracted to sin, lawlessness and rebellion against God.

Everyone needs grace – for all have sinned. Second, to live by faith means we recognize that Jesus alone can transform our sinful nature. *Victory over sin does not come by human will alone – victory comes through an empowering relationship with Jesus.* When we open our minds and hearts to the sweet influence of the Holy Spirit, we receive power to be overcomers. Our carnal nature is diminished through the power of the Holy Spirit! Sinners become saints through this miraculous process! Jesus said, **"You must be born again,"** (John 3:7) but a person cannot make himself a "born again Christian." Spiritual rebirth occurs when we become willing to obey the commands of Jesus, because we love and respect Him. However, this is not the end of the process. By allowing the Holy Spirit to install a new heart within us daily, He will make us willing to *gobedo* (to go, to be, to do) as God directs. Jesus promised, **". . . I will put my laws in their minds and write them on their hearts. I will be their God, and they will be my people."** (Hebrews 8:10) **"You are my friends if you do what I command."** (John 15:14)

A Test of Faith

God has carefully designed a final exam for Earth. He will allow Satan and his forces to gain complete control of the world's religious and political systems for a short time. In this way, God will verify who is willing, on pain of severe penalties, to obey His law! Everyone's true motives will be known – all will see who would rather die than obey the devil.

Consider this issue carefully. Circumstances will be so desperate during the Great Tribulation that obeying the Ten Commandments will be impossible except to do so by faith! In other words, the only way to obey Jesus and keep His commandments will be to stand firm by faith on the promises of God. This is why John identified the remnant as follows: **"Then the dragon was enraged at the woman and went off to make war against the rest of her offspring – those who obey God's commandments and hold to the testimony of Jesus."** (Revelation 12:17)

The Third Angel Speaks Loudly

If you doubt that John was talking about the Ten Commandments when he identified the characteristics of the remnant in the previous text, then look at the third and last warning message to be given to the world. John says, **"A third angel followed them** [the first two angels] **and said in a loud voice: 'If anyone worships the beast** [Satan] **and his image and receives his mark on the forehead or on the hand, he, too, will drink of the wine of God's fury, which has been poured full strength into the cup of his wrath. He will be tormented with burning sulfur in the presence of the holy angels and of the Lamb . . .' This calls for patient endurance on the part of the saints who obey God's commandments and remain faithful to Jesus."** (Revelation 14:9-12)

These verses contain the most solemn warning ever presented to the human race. The coming contest will be simple. It is one of submission! Whom will you obey? God has designed the final events in such a way that only those people who live by faith can obey His Ten Commandments. Is it any wonder that Jesus asked when here on Earth: **"... However, when the Son of Man comes, will He find *faith* on the earth?"** (Luke 18:8)

God personally insures that all inhabitants of Earth will hear His third message. It will be powerfully proclaimed by the 144,000 when Satan physically appears on Earth. This message is specifically directed to the followers of the lamb-like beast that comes up out of the Earth. The devil is called the lamb-like beast because he is the imposter of the Lamb. (Revelation 13:11) Let everyone be warned – the devil will claim to be God! Notice the following points:

1. If any person obeys (submits to) the laws of the devil (the lamb-like beast), he or she will be tormented with burning sulfur in the presence of the Lamb of God! (Revelation 14:10)

2. If anyone chooses to receive the tattoo (the mark) of the devil on their right hand or forehead – which will be required in order to buy or sell – he or she will receive God's wrath full strength! (Revelation 13:16-17; 14:9)

3. People who refuse to worship according to the dictates of the devil must be patient in their suffering. Many people will be killed because they refuse to submit to the devil. John identifies them as obeying God's commandments and remaining faithful to Jesus. (Revelation 12:17, 14:12)

Remember, one of the Ten Commandments specifically deals with God's day of worship. Satan knows this, so he has obscured the importance of the fourth commandment and has led the world to worship on days other than the Lord's day. According to the Bible, the Lord's day is *Saturday*, the seventh day of the week. Jesus said, **"... the Son of Man is Lord even of the Sabbath."** (Mark 2:28) What did Jesus mean when He made this remark? The Pharisees had accused Jesus and His disciples of violating the Sabbath for plucking some grain as they walked through a wheat field. After responding to their charge, Jesus concluded by saying, **"the Son of Man is Lord even of the Sabbath."** By this He declared that His actions, as the Creator of the Sabbath, defined what was appropriate and what was not appropriate on the Sabbath! Yes, Jesus is the member of the Godhead who created the world and the Sabbath. (See John 1:1-14; Hebrews 1:1-3.) Soon, God's children will rest in His finished work of salvation.

Reasons to Worship on Sunday

There is no command to worship God on Sunday in all the Bible. When governments make and enforce laws regarding the sacredness of a specific day of worship to appease God, those countries will quickly go from national apostasy to national ruin. For example, shortly after the first four trumpets (within 30 days), I believe the United States will implement regulations regarding the sacredness of Sunday. Yet, Sunday *is not*, nor has it ever been, God's day of worship. The irony is that Sunday laws defy the law of God, specifically the fourth commandment!

Many God-fearing people mistakenly believe that Sunday is the Lord's day. Scholars have produced a number of glossy *reasons* to confirm the error. But, the Bible does not teach that Sunday has replaced the Sabbath as God's day of worship.

Revelation predicts the following events will occur: Laws regarding the worship of God will be enforced. In the United States, Sunday laws will be implemented, due to Catholic and Protestant dominance. Clerics will use selected Bible texts to assure the masses that God wants man to worship on Sunday and to stop profaning "the Lord's Day." Because most Christians already believe that Sunday is the Lord's day, this will seem consistent and appropriate to the *majority*. Since there are only eight texts in the New Testament that even mention the first day of the week, direct biblical support for the sacredness of Sunday will have to come exclusively from *these* verses. Here are the texts:

Matthew 28:1	Mark 16:2	Mark 16:9
Luke 24:1	John 20:1	John 20:19
Acts 20:7	1 Corinthians 16:2	

The texts in Matthew, Mark, Luke and John state Jesus was resurrected on the first day of the week – a well-known fact. However, none of these texts mention anything about the *sacredness* of Sunday. In fact, Luke 23:56 points out that a group of women did not prepare His body for burial on Friday, but instead rested on the Sabbath "according to the commandment." It is obvious from this text that Jesus did not inform His followers that the fourth commandment was going to be made void because of His death.

Since the first six texts simply discuss the resurrection of Jesus, we will investigate the remaining two verses. Please note the absence of any command from God that would support worship on Sunday.

Acts 20:7

Some preachers refer to Acts 20 as evidence to support Sunday worship. They state that the apostles worshiped on Sunday. But notice what it says, **"On the first day of the week we came together to break bread. Paul spoke to the people and, because he intended to leave the next day, kept on talking until midnight."** (Acts 20:7) Now, consider the details within this verse. In Bible times, a day began at sunset and ended the following evening. Since Creation, the rotation of the Earth has produced this unchanging process. (See Genesis 1:5.) The Jews in Christ's time regarded a day from evening to evening and kept the Sabbath from Friday sundown to Saturday sundown. (In fact, this practice remains intact among Jews today.) Compare Luke 23:50-56 with Leviticus 23:32.

So, the timing described in Acts 20:7 is as follows: Paul stayed with the believers at Troas for seven days. (Acts 20:6) On the evening of the first day of the week, at supper time, the believers met to eat supper with Paul and to say goodbye to their friend. Remember, the first day of the week in Paul's time began Sabbath evening at sundown, or what we now call Saturday night. After supper, Paul preached until midnight, or Saturday midnight. A few hours later on Sunday morning, the first day of the week, he left Troas for Assos.

So, Paul met with believers for supper and preached until midnight, Saturday night. Does a farewell supper and a Saturday night meeting change or abrogate the fourth commandment of God? No. Even if Paul chose to worship on Wednesday night, would this make God's law void? No. Only God can make His law void.

Some preachers claim that the term "breaking of bread" indicates Paul's visit was a communion or worship service. Not so. In Luke 24:13-31 Jesus "broke bread" at supper time with His disciples after walking more than seven miles to Emmaus with them. The breaking of bread, even to this day, remains a Middle Eastern custom since bread is often baked so firm that it has to be literally broken in order to be eaten. We know that Jesus "broke bread" on Thursday night with His disciples at Passover and the Emmaus road experience happened in the evening just as Monday was beginning. Why would Jesus conduct a worship service at sundown in Emmaus, as the second day of the week was beginning? Even if it was a worship service, where is God's command to make void His fourth commandment? Certainly not in Acts 20:7.

Paul did not conduct a Sunday service in Troas. Actually, he held a meeting on Saturday night – the first part of the first day of the week in Bible times. This story confuses a lot of people today, because we reckon a day from midnight to midnight. So, if Christians want to follow Paul's example for authority (rather than the Ten Commandments) on the time of worship, they need to worship on Saturday night (sundown to midnight). But still the question remains – where is the Scriptural authority in this text for Sunday observance?

1 Corinthians 16:2

Some Christians argue that Paul insisted on taking offerings for the poor on the first day of the week. Notice: **"Now about the collection for God's people: Do what I told the Galatian churches to do. On the first day of every week, each one of you should set aside a sum of money in keeping with his income, saving it up, so that when I come no collections will have to be made. Then, when I arrive, I will give letters of introduction to the men you approve and send them with your gift to Jerusalem."** (1 Corinthians 16:1-3)

In Paul's day, money was not a common medium of exchange like it is today. Instead, trading was done through a barter system. For example, a person might trade a chicken or something for cloth or pottery. So, Paul instructed the church in Corinth to begin the week with selling or trading some item since it might take all week to conduct an exchange to obtain a sum of currency. Paul wanted to take *money* with him to give to the persecuted believers in Jerusalem. Since Paul would not be able to travel with roosters, goats, pottery and other things of value, he asked that they take care of this matter, **"first thing after the Sabbath."** (Compare with Nehemiah 13:15.) Again, I ask the question, "Does Paul's instruction change or void the fourth commandment of God?" Not at all.

Thoughts on Romans 6

Some Christians suggest that Sunday worship is appropriate because Jesus arose from the dead on Sunday morning, the first day of the week. Yes, the resurrection is important, and the Bible does provide a celebration of the resurrection! It is called *baptism*. Notice what Paul says, **"What shall we say, then? Shall we go on sinning so that grace may increase? By no means! We died to sin; how can we live in it any longer? Or don't you know that all of us who were baptized into Christ Jesus were baptized into his death? We were therefore buried with him through baptism into death in order that, just as Christ was raised from the dead through the glory of the Father, we too may live a new life."** (Romans 6:1-4)

Does baptism change or abrogate the fourth commandment? Not at all. In fact, not one of the eight texts in the New Testament says that the holiness of the seventh day was ever transferred to Sunday!

What was Nailed to the Cross?

Many Christians argue that the Ten Commandments were nailed to the cross. Yet, this argument does not solve the problem. Whatever happens to the fourth commandment, happens to the other nine! If we do away with the fourth commandment that declares the seventh day to be a holy day, we must also do away with the commandment that says adultery is wrong. Paul wrote, **"What shall we say, then? Is the law sin? Certainly not! Indeed I would not have** known what sin was except through the law. For I would not have known what coveting really was if the law had not said, 'Do not covet.' " (Romans 7:7) It certainly does not appear that Paul thought the Ten Commandments were nailed to the cross.

So, what was nailed to the cross? The ceremonies associated with the sanctuary services were nailed to the cross which were a shadow or explanation of the plan of salvation. The key word is *shadow*. Notice what Paul said, **"For in Christ all the fullness of the Deity lives in bodily form, and you have been given fullness in Christ, who is the head over every power and authority . . . When you were dead in your sins and in the uncircumcision of your sinful nature, God made you alive with Christ. He forgave us all our sins, having canceled the written code, with its regulations, that was against us and that stood opposed to us; he took it away, nailing it to the cross . . . Therefore do not let anyone judge you by what you eat or drink, or with regard to a religious festival, a New Moon celebration or a Sabbath day. These are a shadow of the things that were to come; the reality, however, is found in Christ. Do not let anyone who delights in false humility and the worship of angels disqualify you for the prize . . . ."** (Colossians 2:9-18)

If you look at these verses carefully, you will see that Paul is discussing the regulations regarding *religious feasts, New Moon observances and Sabbath days*. The Sabbath day that Paul is referring to is not *the* Sabbath day of the fourth commandment. Rather, the term "Sabbath days" in this context apply to Sabbath "feast days," such as the Passover or the Day of Atonement. (Leviticus 16:30-31) Certain feast days fell on different days of the week (like our birthday) because they occurred on the same date each year. These feast days were considered special Sabbaths of rest that pointed forward to different aspects of the death and ministry of Jesus. For example, the Passover not only reminded the Jews of deliverance from Egypt, it also pointed forward to the time when the Passover Lamb – Jesus Christ – would die so everyone could be delivered from the bondage of sin!

The Jews confused the Ten Commandment law of God with the laws of Moses, much like we do today. The Jews did not understand the relationship between the moral law (written by God's finger) and the ceremonial laws (written by Moses' hand). One law was permanent, and the other was temporary. The greater law, written by God Himself, was kept inside the ark. This is why the ark was often called the ark of the covenant. (The Ten Commandments are the basis of God's covenant with man. This covenant says, **"If you choose to obey me, I will be your God."** Deuteronomy 30:9-11) The lesser law of Moses, containing ceremonial rules, was kept in a pocket on the outside of the ark. (See Deuteronomy 10:1,2; 31:26.)

Other Objections

Some Christians use Romans 14 to prove that it does not matter which day of the week we use to worship God. Notice the text: **"Accept him whose faith is weak, without** passing judgment on disputable matters. One man's faith allows him to eat everything, but another man, whose faith is weak, eats only vegetables. The man who eats everything must not look down on him who does not, and the man who does not eat everything must not condemn the man who does, for God has accepted him. Who are you to judge someone else's servant? To his own master he stands or falls. And he will stand, for the Lord is able to make him stand. One man considers one day more sacred than another; another man considers every day alike. Each one should be fully convinced in his own mind. He who regards one day as special, does so to the Lord. He who eats meat, eats to the Lord, for he gives thanks to God; and he who abstains, does so to the Lord and gives thanks to God. For none of us lives to himself alone and none of us dies to himself alone. If we live, we live to the Lord; and if we die, we die to the Lord. So, whether we live or die, we belong to the Lord. For this very reason, Christ died and returned to life so that he might be the Lord of both the dead and the living. You, then, why do you judge your brother? Or why do you look down on your brother? For we will all stand before God's judgment seat." (Romans 14:1-10)

The context of these verses does not imply that we can worship God whenever we feel like it. No, this text addresses a specific problem that early Roman Christians had to deal with; namely, the religious customs of the Jews. In other words, if a new believer in Jesus felt he needed to observe Passover, Paul did not condemn the new believer except to say that his faith was weak. Also, if the new believer could not consciously eat meat purchased in the marketplace for fear it had not been killed correctly or that it had been offered before idols, Paul's counsel was to leave him alone! (The Jews would not purchase nor eat meat unless it was killed according to Mosaic code. Leviticus 19:26) Today, many clerics use this text as support for Sunday worship, although I seriously doubt they will use it when they seek the exaltation of Sunday through the enforcement of law.

In another attempt to support Sunday observance, some Christians say that Pentecost came on Sunday the year that Christ died. Since the Holy Spirit was poured out on Sunday, they believe this affirms that Sunday is God's holy day. However, this proves nothing because Pentecost has always fallen on Sunday – ever since the Exodus. The wavesheaf offering was made on the first Sunday after Passover and Pentecost, 50 days (counting inclusively) always occurred on Sunday. (Leviticus 23). So, the annual Pentecost feast occurred on Sunday for more than a millennium before Jesus came to Earth. Does this make the fourth commandment void? No, of course not – and the teachings of Jesus prove it.

Last, some clerics claim that nine of the Ten Commandments are mentioned in the New Testament, but the fourth commandment is missing. Does the absence of the fourth commandment prove it is void or does its absence affirm the assumption of New Testament writers that the Sabbath remained intact without question? Paul clears this up *in the New Testament* by saying, **"There remains, then, a Sab-**

bath-rest for the people of God; for anyone who enters God's rest also rests from his own work, just as God did from his." (Hebrews 4:9,10) Can it be stated any clearer?

Which is the Greatest Law?

As you might expect of a legalistic society, the Jews loved to argue about their laws. An expert lawyer even challenged Jesus with a test to see which law was the greatest! (Matthew 22:34-40) I believe the spirituality of the Jews degenerated into a great legal system of darkness, because they generally misunderstood the purpose of God's laws. (Matthew 23:2-15)

When Paul began to explain the purposes and relationships between the ceremonial laws and God's moral law, you can understand the Jewish hatred exercised against him. Paul claimed that the laws of Moses had expired and this was more than the Jews could tolerate! Paul was imprisoned and eventually beheaded for his convictions. (Acts 21:27-36)

Paul is very explicit in Colossians 2. He points out that the laws nailed to the cross were laws regarding the *shadows* of the real thing. The ceremonial laws requiring the observance of new moons, Sabbath feasts and the sacrifice of lambs became unnecessary because the Lamb of God had died and the shadow of salvation was now open to full view. In other words, ceremonial laws were temporary until their meaning was fulfilled. Moral laws are not temporary, because moral love never ends. One law was written on paper; the other on stone. One law was penned by man; the other, by God. Doesn't this say something about their enduring nature?

Consider Paul's dilemma. How do you get the Jewish nation to understand the distinction between the ceremonial laws and God's Ten Commandments? What a challenge! A proper understanding of Christ and His death would mean they must eliminate the tradition of sacrificing animals that was established more than 1,400 years earlier. It is easy to understand why the Jewish leaders did not like his words. (See 2 Corinthians 11:24-26.) We have, in essence, the same problem today. How can a nation change from a tradition of Sunday observance to Saturday observance without much distress?

Paul is very clear in Hebrews 10 and Galatians 3 and 4 that ceremonies never brought salvation to the Jews in the first place; rather, they were temporary and designed to teach *how* salvation occurs! Paul is also clear that obeying the Ten Commandments cannot produce salvation, because salvation only comes by faith! The problem today is that most Christians think that faith and grace make the law unnecessary. Does love between husband and wife eliminate the necessity for fidelity? No. Neither does living together make two individuals married. The relationship between love and obedience is simple. God grants salvation to everyone who becomes willing to do His will. He does not grant salvation to us on our ability to do His will. We demonstrate our willingness by receiving strength from God to do what He wants. Paul understood this process. (See Romans 7.) In fact, all through his life – and He was converted *after* Christ lived upon Earth – Paul faithfully observed the seventh-day Sabbath. (See Acts 13:44; 16:13; 17:2; 18:4,11.) Even more,

Jesus Himself, called attention to the fact that the seventh-day Sabbath would remain sacred years after His ascension! (Matthew 24:20)

We Cannot Break One Commandment

If we take the position that Jesus nailed the fourth commandment to the cross, then we must conclude that He also nailed the other nine to the cross also. This essential issue will become an important distinction between people who love God and those who rebel against Him. The Ten Commandments are nonnegotiable. They stand as a *unit* representing God's revealed will. God Himself wrote the Ten Commandments. They were written on two tables of stone because they are *based* on two enduring principles: love to God and love to man. The first four commandments explain how we are to love God. The last six commandments explain how we are to love our neighbor. One final point: Maturity in Christ begins when we acknowledge the binding claims of God's law, recognize our great weakness and place our faith in Jesus so that we can fulfill His law through His indwelling power.

Paul knew that all Ten Commandments were intact. He said, **"For I would not have known what it was to covet if the law had not said, 'Do not covet.' "** (Romans 7:7) James also acknowledged the existence of the Ten Commandments when he wrote, **"If you really keep the royal law found in Scripture, 'Love your neighbor as yourself,' you are doing right! But if you show favoritism, you sin and are convicted by the law as lawbreakers. For whoever keeps** the whole law and yet stumbles at just one point is guilty of breaking all of it. For he who said, 'Do not commit adultery,' also said, 'Do not murder.' If you do not commit adultery but do commit murder, you have become a lawbreaker." (James 2:8-11)

James' comments bring us to an important and fundamental conclusion regarding the royal law, the King's law. He says we must obey *all* the commandments. If we break one, we are guilty of breaking them all, because the King's law is only fulfilled by love. We must first love God with all our heart, mind and soul and then, our neighbor as ourselves. How should our love for God be expressed? Jesus said, "If you love me, you will obey what I command." (John 14:15)

Keeping the Sabbath holy will not save anyone. Mandating Saturday laws will not save anyone either! This is why the final exam for the human race is carefully designed *by God to test our relationship* with Jesus: The basis of salvation is faith. Faith is doing what God requires at any cost. Faith is a central requirement for eternal life. As end-time events occur, every visible means of human survival will be cut off and God's people must have great faith in order to obey Him. For most people, it is difficult to have faith in God now. If it is hard to have faith now, what will it be like when our lives are threatened?

Unholy War

Consider this: The devil will lead the world to rebel against God's truth. He will unite the world to worship on a day that stands in direct opposition to the law of God. He will be sure that stringent laws are enacted that will mandate all people to worship as he dictates. (Revelation 13:15-17) The devil will set himself up before the world as the living God. He will receive worship only God deserves and exult in his deception. Paul says, **"He [Satan] opposes and exalts himself over everything that is called God or is worshiped, and even sets himself up in God's temple, proclaiming himself to be God."** (2 Thessalonians 2:4) This prediction will be fulfilled soon after the fifth trumpet sounds.

The Sixth Trumpet

This trumpet will be a global war which Satan initiates to force all nations to submit to a one-world government. God permits Satan to conduct this war at just the right time. Notice what John says, **"The sixth angel blew his trumpet . . . and the four angels (bound at the great river Euphrates) who had been kept ready for this very hour and day and month and year were released to kill a third of mankind. The number of mounted troops was two hundred million. I heard their number . . . A third of mankind was killed by the three plagues of fire, smoke and sulfur that came out of their mouths. The rest of mankind that were not killed by these plagues still did not repent of the work of their hands . . . nor of their murders, their magic arts, their sexual immorality or their thefts."** (Revelation 9:13-21)

What Satan cannot achieve through deceit, he accomplishes through force. Force is always the last resort of false religion. The sixth trumpet war will involve all nations of the world. Satan will direct his followers within each nation to take control of their respective nations. Some people will oppose the heavy demands of the devil and will resist his leadership. This should not surprise anyone for there has always been a segment in society that refuses to worship God. A global civil war will result. Citizens will fight among themselves – Americans fighting Americans, Africans fighting Africans, Europeans fighting Europeans, etc.

God's angels will hold back Satan's political advances until the gospel has reached almost every person. Then, this war will accomplish two things. First, warfare will force everyone to finally choose which "Lamb" they will obey – the one on Earth claiming to be God, or the Lamb who will soon come in the clouds of glory. Second, the war will reveal who the remnant are! They will clearly stand out from the rest of the world.

Antichrist Reigns as God

By the end of the sixth trumpet war, everyone will have made their decision. Many will obey and worship the devil to survive even though they know it is wrong. They will choose the mark of the beast rather than choose to live by faith. Understand this point: If our obedience is not based on faith in Jesus, no one can stand the test of truth. In the future, millions will compromise their religious beliefs; they will receive the mark of the beast so they can buy food and conduct business. John says of the wicked, **"The rest of**

mankind that was not killed [in the war] **did not repent of their** [evils]." (Revelation 9:20-21)

People who receive the mark of the beast will commit open rebellion against the law of God. By the sixth trumpet war, all people on Earth will have made their decision and nothing more can be done to save humanity. Consequently, the door to salvation closes in Heaven and Jesus concludes His mediatorial ministry on behalf of the people of Earth. Then, the seventh trumpet sounds. It is an announcement that salvation has ended and the time has come for the seven last plagues to begin. An earthquake, greater than the one marking the beginning of the Great Tribulation, will occur. This huge global earthquake and the spectacular scenes in the heavens will announce that the offer of salvation to human beings is finished. Every decision will have been made.

Only the Faith–full Will Survive

Standing firm for truth, regardless of the cost, will be the all-encompassing test. Millions of people will die for their faith, others may survive. But, John is very clear – Babylon's forces will kill a large number of God's people. Mercifully, when the seventh trumpet sounds, God will bring martyrdom to an end. (Daniel 12:1) Can you, like Job, say, **"Though He slay me, yet will I hope in Him"**? (Job 13:15) A real testing time is just before us. The test reveals your *faith*. Will you stand firm even if everyone in your family joins the ranks of the enemy?

What About Today?

I am often asked how a person can reconcile the nearness of these events with everyday decisions in life. For example, what does a person do about plans for college, marriage, building or buying a new home, the expansion of a business, retirement savings, career requirements, etc.? I only know of one response to this question. Earnestly seek God for wisdom. He has promised to direct you. As you patiently seek Him, God will show you just what He wants. (Proverbs 3:5-6) So, learn to live by faith now. Keep His Sabbath holy. Put your confidence in God and watch what He will do for you. The ultimate test of having a relationship with Jesus is being able to hear His voice. Jesus said, **"My sheep listen to my voice; I know them, and they follow me."** (John 10:27)

Chapter 6
A Dramatic Rescue by Jesus

This little book draws to an end with a review of the gospel and an invitation. Reviewing the eternal gospel is necessary because it gives us an all-or-nothing proposition. Before the seventh trumpet concludes, all of us will either accept or reject the gospel of Jesus. Some people often try to avoid difficult decisions by putting them far into the background of consciousness. They say, "I will think about this tomorrow." However, postponement is really a decision, too. Suppose you were a young man who asked your sweetheart to marry you right away. Any answer other than "yes" is actually a "no," isn't it? The danger with postponement is that it "candy coats" our rejection until we are trapped by our own inaction. In the case of the gospel, we must listen to the Holy Spirit today. We must be "born again" and we cannot accomplish this on our own. Only through the ministry of the Holy Spirit can we obtain the desire to change our carnal nature. Therefore, it is important to remember that there is a limit to the Holy Spirit's promptings – He will not work with us forever. (Hebrews 3:7-15)

If the Holy Spirit has impressed you that this message is important, you need to restudy it carefully for two reasons. First, your understanding will increase 100% the second time you go through it. Details will become much clearer and more meaningful. Second, now that you understand the contents of Revelation, you need to find an interested friend and share this message. **"The Spirit and the bride say, 'Come!' And let him who hears say, 'Come!' Whoever is thirsty, let him come; and whoever wishes, let him take the free gift of the water of life."** (Revelation 22:17)

The Proclamation of the Gospel

The full gospel must reach every person before Jesus comes. John said, **"Then I saw another angel flying in midair, and he had the eternal gospel to proclaim to those who live on the Earth – to every nation, tribe, language and people."** (Revelation 14:6) Jesus said, **"And this gospel of the kingdom will be preached in the whole world as a testimony to all nations, and then the end will come."** (Matthew 24:14) The question is, "What is the gospel, and who will help spread it?"

What is the Gospel?

In two sentences, the eternal gospel is this: All of us have sinned; therefore, God's law condemns us to death – but Jesus took our place and paid the price for our sins. If we put our faith in Jesus and surrender to His commandments, we will be saved. Look at salvation from God's perspective. Many people honestly live up to all they know to be right and Jesus understands this. In His great mercy, He accepts those people who are sincere in heart and do not know or understand the great truths of the gospel. *Jesus does not hold a person responsible for truth he does not know or cannot know.* On the contrary, James tells us that sin is held against us when we know better and then refuse to do it! **"Anyone, then, who knows the good he ought to do and doesn't do it, sins."** (James 4:17) The Lord loves the people of Earth with a love beyond human understanding. Those living up to all they know to be right glorify God and He is pleased with them. Peter says, **"For the eyes of the Lord are on the righteous and his ears are attentive to their prayer, but the face of the Lord is against those who do evil."** (1 Peter 3:12) Because God's truth has been so obscured from most of the world by Satan's devices, Jesus will soon awaken the world to hear the gospel. People who are sincere in heart will rejoice to learn more and they will embrace the truth as it continues to unfold. Thus, God will gather the remnant out of all religious systems into one body under the leadership of Jesus. Jesus said, **"I have other sheep that are not of this sheep pen. I must bring them also. They too will listen to my voice, and there shall be one flock and one shepherd."** (John 10:16)

So, the net effect of the gospel in the last days will be to unify those who hear the voice of Jesus into one last group called the remnant. God will accomplish this during the time-period of the trumpets by separating sheep from goats. (Matthew 25:31-46) People will either receive the gospel and by faith, obey the commandments of Jesus as the three angel's messages command, or they will reject the gospel and eventually choose the mark of the beast. There will be no middle ground. The rapid sequence of events, coupled with rigorous laws requiring disobedience to the law of God will push everyone into a rapid decision.

What Must I do to be Saved?

One of Satan's most powerful deceptions has two sides. The devil has led many people to believe that salvation comes either through obedience to God (as in human performance) or by intellectual assent to what is true. Satan's trickery is very subtle. He can actually make evil people think they are righteous! For example, Satan led the Pharisees to believe they were righteous even though they were far away from the kingdom. Jesus said to them, **". . . on the outside you appear to people as righteous but on the inside you are full of hypocrisy and wickedness."** (Matthew 23:28)

From their point of view, the Pharisees believed they were righteous and could see nothing wrong with themselves. So, how can a person know if his life is acceptable to God? Jesus said, **". . . every good tree bears good fruit, a good tree cannot bear bad fruit, but a bad tree bears bad fruit, and a bad tree cannot bear good fruit."** (Matthew 7:17,18) Religious people often say one thing and do another. So, we must test ourselves from time to time to see if we are in Christ! Paul wrote, **"Examine yourselves to see whether you are in the faith; test yourselves. Do you not realize that Christ Jesus is in you – unless, of course, you fail the test?"** (2 Corinthians 13:5)

How do we test ourselves? To evaluate whether Jesus really is in our hearts, let us look at two extreme examples. The first example describes a religious type of person called "workers." These individuals are *working* their way to Heaven, but do not know it. The second group of people is called "thinkers." This group *thinks* they have salvation because they agree with the Bible.

The Workers

"Workers" say, "I am saved by faith," even though they are actually working their way to Heaven. People who have this characteristic are usually identified by zealous and/or rigorous obedience to the teachings or ideals of their denomination/God. Workers tend to see sin as acts of *commission*, that is, sins or wrongful deeds acted out. To live within the rules is very important to these people. In their hearts, they are confident that they are saved because they are obedient to all the rules. They look at themselves and see very little wrong. Workers, in day-to-day living, regard obedience as the *primary process* through which salvation occurs, even though they may say, "Salvation comes by faith!"

The Jewish religion at the time of Christ typifies this great deception. Spiritual pride blinded the Jews and they could not see anything wrong with themselves! Like the Pharisees, the worker-types often criticize "outsiders" who break the rules, but they rarely speak about their own sins of *omission*. Jesus said to the Pharisees, **"Woe to you Pharisees, because you give God a tenth of your mint, rue and all other kinds of garden herbs, but you neglect justice and** the love of God. You should have practiced the latter without leaving the former undone . . . And you experts in the law, woe to you, because you load people down with burdens they can hardly carry, and you yourselves will not lift one finger to help them." (Luke 11:42,46)

The coming tribulation will easily overtake the workers. Workers will not be able to obey God in the days ahead, for civil laws will become so strict and the penalty so great that obedience will be almost impossible! (Remember how Hitler threatened the German people – if anyone helped a Jew, that person would be punished in the same manner as the Jews.) In the future, to avoid suffering and the possibility of death, workers will have no other option but to submit to the laws of Babylon! Yes, I assume that some of the workers, because of religious pride will stand stiffly for what they believe. But, after they are gone, what will their family members do? When the great religious organizations of the world merge as a result of the massive destruction caused by the seven trumpets, whose rules will the workers follow? Without strong faith in God, no one can withstand Babylon. (Revelation 13:8)

The great tragedy surrounding the worker deception is how the devil makes obedience the object of religion and not the means to have a saving relationship with Jesus. Jesus said of the Jews, "They worship me in vain; their teachings are but rules taught by men. You have let go of the commands of God and are holding on to the traditions of men." (Mark 7:7,8)

The Thinkers

At the other end of the pendulum, Satan has a counterfeit about salvation that is equally dangerous and perhaps more widely received than the worker concept. In brief, this counterfeit maintains that if you *believe* you are saved, you are saved! In general terms, this doctrine teaches that obedience to the Ten Commandments is unnecessary; even more, obedience to the fourth commandment is an insult to God's grace. Adherents to this doctrine believe the Christian is under grace and not under the law, as if grace makes the law null and void. The thinkers say the words: "Jesus is Lord," and profess to love their neighbors.

Many believe they have salvation simply by "agreeing" that Jesus died on Calvary. But how can our agreement with historical fact bring salvation? James wrote, **"You believe that there is one God. Good! Even the demons believe that – and shudder."** (James 2:19)

I label these people "thinkers" because they *think* they receive salvation by some mental process. Thinkers tend to enjoy their religion more than workers because their religion is people-oriented. Workers tend to be more judgmental and critical of behavior, whereas thinkers are more generous and casual about their behavior. Thinkers claim that God's stringent rules, the Ten Commandments, were done away with at the cross; therefore, anything socially acceptable is acceptable to God. The thinker's gospel has few requirements and they say, "He accepts us as we are." Thinkers conclude that righteousness comes with intellectual assent, so just believe you are saved and join a church. The heart of the thinker's gospel is the golden rule, "Do unto your neighbor as you would have him do unto you."

The thinker's gospel, like the worker's gospel, has some good points, but both fall short of God's design. The essence of true religion is to first love God with heart, mind and soul, and your neighbor as yourself. But what is love for God? James asked the same question, **"What good is it, my brothers, if a man claims to have faith but has no deeds? Can such faith save him? Suppose a brother or sister is without clothes and daily food. If one of you says to him, 'Go, I wish you well; keep warm and well fed,' but does nothing about his physical needs, what good is it? In the same way, faith by itself, if it is not accompanied by action, is dead. But someone will say, 'You have faith; I have deeds.' Show me your faith without deeds, and I will show you my faith by what I do . . . You see that a person is justified by what he does and not by faith alone."** (James 2:14-24)

Summary

Certain extreme characteristics found in thinkers and workers have been presented to demonstrate the kinds of behavior that such theological processes produce. What we *do* reveals what we really *believe*!

Satan has cleverly counterfeited the gospel of the workers and thinkers by using *partial* truth in each case! So, do not be fooled. Both doctrines are deadly. The simple truth about salvation is this: Salvation by faith means a complete surrender of the will to Jesus. It means to be all that God asks, do all that God requires, and go wherever Jesus directs. True salvation produces a life of action. Obedience comes as a result of experiencing salvation – not salvation as a result of obedience. Look closely at Hebrews 11 and you will observe that each person in this Hall of Faith was obedient to God's commands! Paul says of Abraham, **"By faith Abraham, when God tested him, offered Isaac as a sacrifice. He who had received the promises was about to sacrifice his one and only son, even though God had said to him, 'It is through Isaac that your offspring will be reckoned.'** [Genesis 22] **Abraham reasoned that God could raise the dead, and figuratively speaking, he did receive Isaac back from death."** (Hebrews 11:17-19) That old gospel favorite by James Sammis and Daniel Towner, "Trust and Obey," summarizes the gospel message very well:

> "When we walk with the Lord
> In the light of His Word,
> What a glory He sheds on our way!
> While we do His good will,
> He abides with us still,
> And with all who will trust and obey.
> Trust and obey,
> For there's no other way
> To be happy in Jesus,
> But to trust and obey."

Sound Asleep?

Many Christians scoff at the suggestion that the Lord will return this decade. They see no reason for all the excitement. They say, "All things continue as usual – why all the fuss?" These people are content in their spiritual poverty. They have no idea about the events coming upon the Earth, and even worse, they do not want to hear about it! They like religious media programming – entertainment that features talented singers and gifted speakers with clever ideas. They do not want to hear about the wrath of God or the cross that we must bear. Thus, Satan has convinced many within the Christian church that they are either safe from the tribulation or that life will continue as usual until Jesus returns. Unfortunately, these deceptions are widely accepted.

Those who understand the everlasting gospel do not focus on gloom or doom. Instead, these people focus on the greatest and most awesome event in Earth's history, the revelation of Jesus at the Second Coming. They also know that a testing time, a purifying time, precedes the Second Coming. They know about the future rise of Babylon and the appearing of Satan claiming to be God. These people know about the "unholy war" that will be waged against them. And yes, they know that their faith will be fully tested. Yet, they are positive about their relationship with Jesus, which gives them peace in their hearts. These people are committed to being "overcomers." They claim God's promises daily and "have ears to hear what the Spirit is saying to them." They walk by faith and will be prepared for a mighty work when the trumpets sound.

Worship God

Satan has led most of the world to deny the importance of God's seventh day Sabbath. Friday is the day of worship for more than one billion Moslems. About 25 million Jews recognize Saturday as God's holy day (but a Sabbath without Jesus is like cake with no icing), and one and a half billion Christians (all Christians combined: Catholics, Protestants, Greek Orthodox, Anglican, etc.) believe in the sacredness of Sunday. Nearly three billion people have no regard for the sacredness of any special day of the week.

It should be clear that worshiping on God's holy day does not, nor can it ever, bring salvation to a person. For example, if an alien sneaks into a country and keeps all of the laws, he still does not become a citizen by obeying the laws. Rather, an alien becomes a citizen by *submitting* to the immigration process. Part of the process involves taking an oath of allegiance to the laws of that nation. Salvation, in a similar way, comes when we submit our lives to Jesus. This means that we are willing to go, to be and to do as He directs (*go be do*). We put our will aside and place Jesus on the throne of our heart. Then, Jesus directs us. Faith involves obedience to all Ten Commandments. Thus, John identified the remnant as those people having the faith of Jesus; otherwise, they could not obey the commandments of God. (Revelation 12:17; 13:10; 14:12)

The most wonderful part of God's salvation during the end-time is this: During the Great Tribulation, God is going to give every faith-full person the greatest gift possible. This gift is a completely new nature. It is a nature that loves to render obedience to God – a nature free of rebellion – a nature that is naturally opposed to sin. In short, Jesus is going to bestow His righteous nature on those who want it. (Hebrews 8:10,11)

Get Prepared

If the Bible teaches anything, it teaches that salvation comes by faith in Jesus. God knows our fears are great. God knows we have no strength, glory or righteousness. God knows that man is made of the dust of the ground, but He also loves us so much that He gave His only Son to die in our place. Yes, the events before us will be frightening and overwhelming. Yes, the coming tribulation will be greater than anything the world has ever known. But, the presence of God will never be closer and His peace never more valuable. So, give yourself to Him right now. Believe on the name of our Lord, Jesus Christ. Live a life of faith – tell the Lord that you are willing to be, to do and to go as He commands – and when He comes, YOU will be saved. The Lord, Jesus Christ, guarantees it.

Appendix
The Prophetic Importance of 1994

I believe the year 1994, was and still is, prophetically significant. This appendix provides information that will illustrate the apocalyptic significance of the calendar year 1994 and why this specific point in time is important to the end-time story. When studying apocalyptic prophecy, the student needs to understand that two types of time periods exist within the end-time sequence of events: Jubilee calendation (a day for a year) and literal time.

Every student of Daniel and Revelation faces this challenge – where do the prophetic time-periods belong? The prophet Daniel wrote about 70 weeks, 2,300 days, 1,290 days, 1,335 days, 7 times, and two time-periods called, "a time, times and half a time." Likewise, John, in the book of Revelation, wrote about 1,000 years, 42 months, two time-periods of 1,260 days, five months, one hour, half an hour, and one time-period called, "a time, times and half a time." Obviously, the conclusions that a person reaches about prophecy impact the placement of the biblical time-periods. A key issue that needs to be clarified when calculating time-periods in Daniel and Revelation is whether the time period should be reckoned in literal units of time or interpreted according to a day/year principle. (The day/year principle will be discussed shortly.)

A number of prophetic expositors believe that all time-periods should be reckoned consistently, i.e., all time-periods should be reckoned according to the day/year principle or they should all be reckoned as literal. In other words, time-periods within Bible prophecy should not be mixed. Such a position frustrates and obstructs the integral harmony required of Bible prophecy. For example, the 70 weeks of Daniel 9 cannot logically fit on a historical time-line if the expositor insists that the time-period is 70 *literal* weeks. On the other hand, it does not seem possible that the coming 42 months of Revelation 13 represent 1,260 literal years *after* the deadly wound is healed or Christ's return would be so far into the future that it would be irrelevant for the next 25 generations. Nor is it logical to consider the 1,000 years in Revelation 20 to be a day for a year because that would make the millennium 360,000 years in length.

My study of the time-periods and supporting Scripture has led me to conclude that some time-periods should be reckoned as literal and other time-periods according to the day/year principle. For example, the 70 weeks in Daniel 9 require the day/year principle (70 weeks representing 490 solar years), whereas the 42 months in Revelation 13 are 42 literal months.

My assertion that some time-periods are literal and other periods reckoned according to the day/year principle creates a problem. The problem is identifying which time-periods are literal and which are day/year. Since we know prophetic study is not a matter of "private interpretation" (an arbitrary method to justify a personal perspective), a private interpretation of these time periods is not appropriate. There must be self-evident rules that somehow establish how God, the Author of these time-periods, reckons them.

One rule of design that I have found to operate consistently is this: "The absence or presence of the Jubilee calendar determines how prophetic time is to be reckoned." If the Jubilee calendar is operating, God reckons time according to the Jubilee calendar – that is, a day for a year. If the Jubilee calendar is not operating, prophetic time-periods should be reckoned as literal time.

Not Time-setting

As I understand it, the Jubilee calendar began to operate in 1437 B.C. and it ceased to operate 70 Jubilee cycles later in 1994. The basis for this claim will be presented shortly. In regards to timing, let me make one point perfectly clear – contrary to what many have said about me, I do not know, nor have I ever claimed to know the date our Lord will return. However, a Bible student cannot exclude the study of time-periods from Bible prophecy. Therefore, we should carefully consider the time-periods that God has given, just as the prophets of old searched for understanding in the prophecies concerning the coming Messiah. Notice what Peter said about time-study: **"Concerning this salvation, the prophets, who spoke of the grace that was to come to you, searched intently and with the greatest care,** *trying to find out the time* **and circumstances to which the Spirit of Christ in them was pointing when he predicted the sufferings of Christ and the glories that would follow."** (1 Peter 1:10,11; emphasis mine)

Seven Millenniums?

Bible students have long anticipated that sin would soon come to an end. For example, the Bible says that a time is coming when sin will be destroyed. (Isaiah 51:6; Revelation 20) If sin is to be destroyed in the future, we must conclude that God has set a limit for the duration of sin. What is that limit? Is it 7,000 years?

I am convinced that from the first day of creation, the primary purpose of time has been to mark the timely fulfillment of God's purposes. God foreknew the existence of sin. When He made the weekly cycle, He gave us a "veiled" clue about His plans and purposes. Did not God's foreknowledge anticipate the rise of sin? Certainly! Some people claim that God just chose to create a seven day week. However, I believe God is deliberate and purposeful in everything He does. So, what value does time have within the dimension of timeless eternity? The value of time (as defined on this planet) is this: God uses time to reveal Earth's progress toward the consummation of His plans. The very presence of hours, days, weeks, months and years is important not only within man's planning, it is important within our Creator's planning. In fact, one reason why I believe the weekly cycle stands as a "veiled" clue about God's timing is that God often creates prophetic time-periods that confirm the presence of the weekly cycle. For example, the mention of 42 months (3.5 years), 1,260 days (3.5 years) and a time, times and half a time (3.5 years) are "half-week" units. Does God's deliberate creation and use of these time-periods suggest the presence of the weekly cycle as a template? I think so. His repetitive use of 3.5 units throughout prophecy suggests the presence of 7 units.

This brings up an important question. Are the 1,000 years mentioned in Revelation 20 a random number of years or are they a carefully designated period of time? I believe this coming millennium described in Revelation 20 will be the seventh and final millennium that sin will exist in the universe. For the saints, the seventh millennium will be a sabbatical rest from the works of sin! Then finally, at the end of the 1,000 years, sin and sinners will be completely destroyed and the universe will be clean.

Weekly Cycle

The seven-day week, which the Creator established during creation week, is not synchronous with the celestial motions of the sun, moon or stars – nor any known biological cycle. We can learn about God by studying nature, but man could not know about a seven-day cycle called the week without God's direct revelation. We can calculate the exact length of a day, lunar month or solar year, but how could people from all cultures determine a week's period to be seven days if God had not invented it? The phenomenon of the weekly cycle is transoceanic – a cross culture witness. It indicates that all mankind has the same Creator and that God created the world in seven days. In fact, more than 200 ancient languages identify the seventh day as a day of rest. I suspect that the weekly cycle provides a template for the amount of time God has allotted to redeem man. Here's how:

The first six days of God's Creation week parallel six millennial days of sin's destructive effect. During Creation week, God's creative works became more beautiful, complex and intelligent as He progressed toward the seventh day (the Sabbath). In fact, Sabbath, the crowning work of Creation, can only be appreciated and understood by the highest living form of creation – Man. Conversely, sin has followed a similar, but inverse effect. As we approach the seventh millennium, sin becomes more destructive, complicated and nonsensical. Man cannot extricate himself from the cancer of sin. The more sinful and degenerate man becomes, the less he appreciates and understands his Maker's will. Contrast the difference. God's process is ascending, noble and beautiful. Sin's process is descending, degenerate and despicable. The point behind this sad parallel is that even in the degradation of sin, God's Sabbath rest remains. Whether it is understood or not, respected or not, man cannot rescind or make God's weekly Sabbath rest void for it points to the millennial sabbatical rest, when the saints will rest *from* the works of sin. (See Hebrews 4.) Sin is not eliminated from the universe until the end of the millennium. (Revelation 20:15)

The 6,000th Year

When does the 6,000th year occur? No one knows for sure and the Bible does not resolve the question. However, the genealogies of the Bible do provide some insight. But, genealogies have problems, too. Early manuscripts vary. Even at best, there is a margin of error. However, there appears to be evidence enough to know the "time zone" of the 6,000th year. It appears that A.D. 2000 is the earliest possible candidate for the 6,000th year and the latest candidate is about A.D. 2017. Keep in mind that this range is based on Bible records. The genealogies recorded in Genesis 5:1-32; 7:11; and 11:1-32 are shown on Figure 1 and Figure 2 (on following page):

Time Period between Creation and the Flood		
Creation	Flood	Father's Age at Son's Birth
Adam	Seth	130
Seth	Enosh	105
Enosh	Kenan	90
Kenan	Mahalalel	70
Mahalalel	Jared	65
Jared	Enoch	162
Enoch	Methuselah	65
Methuselah	Lamech	187
Lamech	Noah	182
Noah	The Flood	600th Year
Total Years from Man's Fall to the Flood		1,656 Years**

Figure 1

Time Period between the Flood and the Exodus		
Flood	Exodus	Father's Age at Son's Birth
The Flood	Arphaxad	2
Arphaxad	Shelah	35
Shelah	Eber	30
Eber	Peleg	34
Peleg	Reu	30
Reu	Serug	32
Serug	Nahor	30
Nahor	Terah	29
Terah	Abraham	70
Abraham	Isaac	100
Isaac	Jacob	60
Jacob	Joseph goes into Egypt	107*
Joseph in Egypt	The Exodus	430* years @ 1437 B.C.
Total Years From the Flood to the Exodus		989 Years**

Figure 2

*Jacob was 107 years old when Joseph was taken to Egypt. It is my understanding that the 430 years of Exodus 12:41 is dated from Joseph's entry into Egypt as a slave. However, some Bible students prefer to date the 430 years from Abraham's call. (Genesis 12:1) If their position is correct and the date of the Exodus is 1437 B.C., then Creation would have to be dated about 3888 B.C. and the 6,000th year of sin would occur between A.D. 2112-2131.

**It is highly unlikely that the first born of each generation was born on the birthday of his ancestor. For example, 21 generations could have a maximum additive error of almost 21 years. Further, no record exists showing how long Adam and Eve lived in the Garden of Eden before they sinned. Thus, the beginning date for the 6,000 years of sin cannot be precisely identified.

Exodus Dating

If we consider the genealogical records of Genesis and the prophetic time-periods listed in Daniel and Revelation, it is possible to calculate a reasonable range on the "time zone" of the 6,000th year. To make our calculations as accurate as possible, the date of the Exodus needs to be determined. This is important because the Jubilee calendar accurately clarifies certain prophetic time-periods and historical dates for the past 3,430 years. I have concluded that only one date can satisfy the date of the Exodus. It is 1437 B.C. Since the Jubilee calendar operates in units of 49 years, if 1437 B.C. is not correct, then the actual date has to be increased or decreased by units of 49 years. In other words, due to the nature of the Jubilee calendar, calculations cannot be off the mark by one or two years, but rather in units of 49 years. (This point will be demonstrated later.) If 1437 B.C. is indeed the date of the Exodus, and if the genealogical numbers in the Hebrew Pentateuch are trustworthy (allowing for some additive error), then Creation week took place about 4103 B.C.

1437 B.C.	The Exodus
+ 989 Years	Time from the Flood to the Exodus
+1,656 Years	Time from Adam's Creation to the Flood
+ 21 Years	Maximum Possible Additive Error
4103 B.C.	The Creation
4000 B.C.	The Beginning of Sin
A.D. 2000	The Earliest Year Possible for the 6,000th Year?

Figure 3

Note: The above dates assume that Adam and Eve lived in the Garden of Eden for about 100 - 110 years before sinning. (Cain and Abel were born after their expulsion from Eden and Seth was born when they were 130 years old.) So, the 100 - 110 years is "within reason" for the future prophetic time-periods in Daniel and Revelation to be fulfilled as early as A.D. 2000.

Seventh Millennium

The seventh millennium is important as a Sabbatical millennium because the promise of entering God's Sabbath-rest still remains. Notice these verses: **"For forty years I was angry with that generation; I said, 'They are a people whose hearts go astray, and they have not known my ways.' So I declared on oath in my anger, 'They shall never enter My rest.' "** (Psalms 95:10-11) Why does God refer to the Promised Land as **"My rest"**? What is the connection between God's seventh-day Sabbath-rest and the Promised Land in the book of Hebrews? This text is important to our study because the Promised Land symbolizes God's seventh-day Sabbath-rest. In other words, the weekly rest of the seventh day was meant to be a sample of the joy that would be found in the Promised Land. Unfortunately, the first generation of Israelites were not faithful and as a result did not enter God's rest. Fifteen hundred years after the Exodus, the apostle Paul understood that the Sabbath-rest of the *eternal* Promised Land was still in the future. Notice what he said, **"There remains, then, a Sabbath-rest for the people of God; for anyone who enters God's rest also rests from his own work, just as God did from his. Let us, therefore, make every effort to enter that rest, so that no one will fall by following their example of disobedience."** (Hebrews 4:9-11)

Is this Sabbath-rest described in Hebrews the seventh-day Sabbath and the seventh millennium? It seems so because in Paul's mind the Sabbath-rest is directly related to God's seventh-day Sabbath. My guess is that the seventh millennium will start and end right on time, just as the seventh-day Sabbath starts and ends on time each week. Space limitations dictate that we leave this section with some thoughts unfinished, but the threads will be picked up in the summary.

Seventy Jubilee Cycles

Because God is neither shallow nor mindless about the things He creates, we should carefully consider the calendar He introduced to Israel just before the Exodus. This calendar is often called the Jubilee calendar. It is built upon a template of the weekly cycle. It is a matrix of seven weeks (or 7's) totaling 49 years. Look at the matrix below and notice that it is one week wide and seven weeks tall (7 by 7):

God's Calendar

	Sun Year	Mon Year	Tue Year	Wed Year	Thu Year	Fri Year	Sab Year
Week 1	1	2	3	4	5	6	7
Week 2	8	9	10	11	12	13	14
Week 3	15	16	17	18	19	20	21
Week 4	22	23	24	25	26	27	28
Week 5	29	30	31	32	33	34	35
Week 6	36	37	38	39	40	41	42
Week 7	43	44	45	46	47	48	49

Figure 4

Now, notice how today's calendar and God's calendar compare:

Today's Calendar		God's Calendar	
1 Decade	= 10 Years	1 Week	= 7 Years
10 Decades	= 100 Years	7 Weeks	= 49 Years
100 Years	= 1 Century	49 Years	= 1 Jubilee Cycle

The Jubilee calendar is particularly important to the study of prophecy. A basic working knowledge of this calendar is necessary to understand why some prophetic time-periods are calculated in "day for a year" units. Ultimately, the Jubilee calendar also helps to confirm the importance of seven millenniums.

At the time of the Exodus, God gave the Israelites a special calendar based on observation. By observing the phases of the Sun and Moon, the ancients could accurately determine the arrival of seasons, the time for planting and harvest, feasts and other religious events. This calendar, called the Jubilee calendar because of the jubilant rejoicing that occurred at its fiftieth year climax, was not based on a series of complex calculations, but instead on simple observation. According to the Jubilee calendar, each new year began with the first new moon *after* the Spring equinox. A new moon also marked the beginning of each new month. (A new moon is a totally dark moon. A full moon is a totally bright moon that occurs fifteen days after the new moon.) The Jubilee calendar was a solar-lunar calendar – meaning that time was not calculated by one heavenly object alone. In this way, when God created the solar-lunar calendar, He solved two important problems. First, by watching for the change of shadows at the Spring equinox, His people could use "dead reckoning" in terms of precise solar positioning. This means they could precisely identify Earth's "Spring" position. (This was no small matter given the understanding of ancient man concerning the orbits of celestial bodies and was especially serious since the nation of Israel was primarily agricultural. Do not underestimate the importance of timely planting.) God also solved a second problem by establishing a solar-lunar calendar. The ancients knew a lunar year (12 lunar months) is actually 10 or 11 days shorter than a solar year. A lunar calendar was not practical because each year the cycle of the moon was very hard to calculate. Since a lunar calendar is not always accurate with respect to the seasons, the ancients used a variety of methods to measure time. For example, the Egyptians, at the time of the Exodus, used a 365 day calendar that was periodically adjusted so that the celebration of their New Year and the planting of crops coincided with Earth's orbit around the Sun. On the other hand, God's solar-lunar calendar was self-correcting every Spring. His calendar was not rendered inaccurate even though some years had 13 months (moons) and others had 12. The Israelites did not observe the Fall-to-Fall Babylonian calendar that marks off three solar years as 37 lunar months until *after* the Babylonian captivity (605-536 B.C.). From then on, the Spring-to-Spring Jubilee calendar was called the "divine calendar" and the Fall Babylonian calendar became the civil calendar.

As a result of God's thoughtful design, the Passover and the Feast of Tabernacles always occurred on a full moon (the 15th day of a lunar month always has a full moon). This was especially helpful since Israelite males often traveled long distances to reach these required feasts in Jerusalem and by the fifteenth day of a lunar month, they could travel by the light of the moon.

Under the Jubilee calendar, each day of the week represented a year. (Leviticus 25:3-8) The weekly cycle was the template for a week of seven years. The first year of each cycle corresponded to the first day of the week, and so forth. (See Figure 4 on page 152.) Contrary to what many people claim, the Jubilee calendar was implemented two weeks *before* the Exodus (Exodus 12:1,2), in the Spring of the year. More details will be provided about this later.

In ancient times, it was the custom for each nation to adopt its own calendar. So, time was often referred to like this: **"In the 15th year of the reign of Tiberius Caesar . . . ."** (Luke 3:1) Because there were multitudes of small nations, numerous calendars existed, which meant there was no common method for evaluating time. In an attempt to rectify this situation, Julius Caesar, in 45 B.C., established the Julian calendar. Prior to his calendar, cross-dating an event was almost impossible. Consider the problems. Pompous kings liked to have time dated according to their rule, but every time a new king ascended to the throne, the calendar started over. You can imagine the problems ancient historians had when trying to identify dates, not to mention the problems modern historians have as they try to date events from the past. As a result, it has become very difficult to accurately date ancient events by archeological records alone.

The Sabbatical Year

God declared that after Israel entered the land He was going to give them, the land itself must observe a Sabbath of rest each seventh year. (Leviticus 25:3-7) This meant that every seventh year the land was to lay fallow. It was not to be planted or harvested. In His divine wisdom, God's intention was to accomplish two important things with the seventh-year Sabbatical. First, by observing a seventh-year sabbatical, Israel would always keep the importance of God's weekly seventh-day Sabbath intact. Second and more importantly, God wanted to test Israel's faith every seventh year to see if they would trust Him and observe His Sabbath years. Some people claim that the Sabbatical was to benefit the land only; however, the facts contradict this claim. The Bible indicates that the sixth or last year of the harvest cycle produced more food than other years! (Leviticus 25:21) In other words, God purposely blessed the sixth year, making the largest crop occur after the soil had been producing for five consecutive years.

The Jubilee Year

The 49th year of a Jubilee cycle was considered a high Sabbatical year because it was the seventh Sabbath year of the cycle. The Jubilee year was the following year or the 50th year, and therefore was a once-per-generation celebration.

(Leviticus 25:8-10) The Jubilee year was also observed as a Sabbatical year, and it marked the completion of a Jubilee cycle, just like a wedding anniversary celebrates the completion of another year of marriage. This may sound strange at first, but the 50th year celebration and the first year of a new cycle happened on the *same* year. For this reason, some people are confused about the length of a Jubilee cycle – whether it is 49 or 50 years in length. God provides a simple solution to this question by using the timing of the Feast of Pentecost. The Feast of Pentecost occurred on the 50th day after seven, seventh-day Sabbaths had passed. (Leviticus 23:15,16) This meant that the 50th day of Pentecost always occurred on the first day of the week. In like manner, the 50th year Jubilee always occurred on the first year (Sunday year) of the new Jubilee cycle. In addition to this point, the unbroken weekly cycle of years confirms that Jubilee cycles were to be reckoned as adjacent units of seven weeks containing 49 years. (See Figure 5 on page 159.)

During the Jubilee year, God also required that all real estate debts be canceled and all land be returned to its original owner. (Homes within cities were excluded.) God did this to remind each generation that the land they possessed was not theirs, but His. (See Leviticus 25:23 and Jeremiah 2:7.) He wanted them to know that they did not earn or deserve the land, but that He had given it to them because He loved them. (It is still the same today. The saints who inherit the New Earth will know they do not deserve the land, but it comes as a gift from God.) One final point, the Israelites were not to plant or harvest their fields during the Jubilee year, for it was a holy Sabbatical year to the Lord, just like the Sabbatical years. (Leviticus 25:11,12)

The Meaning of Rest

We have considered three things. First, the seventh-year Sabbatical rest for the land was a test – would Israel rest from their labor, trust God and allow Him to supply their needs? (Exodus 16:4) Second, the Jubilee year was an extra special test of faith – one Sabbatical year followed another consecutively, and all property outside the cities was to be returned to its original owners. Finally, the observance of these two events were designed to keep the observance of the Jubilee cycle intact. Notice the intimate relationship in God's calendar surrounding the Sabbath. The observance of the seventh-day Sabbath was to keep the weekly cycle intact, and the observance of the Sabbatical years was to keep the weeks of years intact, which in turn was to keep the Jubilee cycles intact.

Consider the following information about the Jubilee calendar: With the exception of the very first Jubilee cycle at the time of the Exodus, each Jubilee cycle contains eight Sabbatical years: seven, seventh-year Sabbaticals, plus the first year, which is the Jubilee year Sabbatical. Also notice that the next Jubilee cycle continues without interrupting the weekly cycle. It is interesting to note that any Sabbatical year is always a function of seven. For example, the Sabbatical year for Week 4 is year number 28 ($7 \times 4 = 28$).

Jubilee Cycle Example

	Sun Year	Mon Year	Tue Year	Wed Year	Thu Year	Fri Year	Sab Year
First Jubilee Cycle							
Week 1	1	2	3	4	5	6	7
Week 2	8	9	10	11	12	13	14
Week 3	15	16	17	18	19	20	21
Week 4	22	23	24	25	26	27	28
Week 5	29	30	31	32	33	34	35
Week 6	36	37	38	39	40	41	42
Week 7	43	44	45	46	47	48	49
Next Jubilee Cycle							
Week 1	50/1	2	3	4	5	6	7
Week 2	8	9	10	11	12	13	14
Week 3	15	16	17	18	19	20	21
Weeks of Years Continue Similarly							

Legend: Jubilee Year ▓ Sabbatical Year ▒

Figure 5

Warning!

What God makes holy, He declares important to man. God does not allow man to treat His holy things with contempt and remain guiltless. God has warned human beings about His wrath and He will punish the human race for willfully trampling on His holy laws. But, understand that if a person tramples on God's holy commands, including the Sabbath, without knowing that he is doing wrong, God does not hold that person accountable – even though he is guilty! (Leviticus 4:13) However, if a person refuses to recognize, admit or learn about God's commands and His holy Sabbath, sooner or later he or she will find himself in serious trouble. Unfortunately, this was the experience of Israel.

When God gave Israel the Jubilee calendar, He made their responsibility clear. He warned, **"But if you will not listen to me and carry out all these commands, and if you reject my decrees and abhor my laws and fail to carry out all my commands and so violate my covenant, then I will do this to you: . . . I will lay waste the land, so that your enemies who live there will be appalled. I will scatter you among the nations and will draw out my sword and pursue you. Your land will be laid waste, and your cities will lie in ruins. Then the land will enjoy its Sabbath years all the time that it lies desolate and you are in the country of your enemies; then the land will rest and enjoy its Sabbaths. All the time that it lies desolate, the land will have the rest it did not have during the Sabbaths you lived in it."** (Leviticus 26:14-35) The penalty for violating the Sabbatical years accurately portrays the value and significance that God placed on them. Violation of the Sabbatical years was severe because God wanted Israel to live by faith. He also wanted Israel to perpetuate His calendar. God initiated the Jubilee calendar two weeks before the Exodus (Exodus 12:2) to designate the beginning of Israel as a nation. Indeed, the annual Passover services were designed to remind Israel of their benevolent Creator.

Jubilees are in the Bible

The silence of Sabbatical or Jubilee celebrations in the Bible leads me to conclude that Israel failed to measure up to God's ideal. In fact, there is only one Jubilee mentioned in all the Bible. It is mentioned twice: Isaiah 37:30 and 2 Kings 19:29. (An oblique reference is found in Ezekiel 7:13) Also, the seventh-year Sabbatical is mentioned twice, once in Jeremiah 34 and also in Nehemiah 10.

God's patience and long-suffering with Israel's backsliding is beyond human understanding. For centuries He tried to get Israel to shape up and accomplish all that He had in mind, but they refused. Over and over, Israel filled up its cup of iniquity and God responded with appropriate punishments. But two incidents in particular could be classified as a point in Israel's history when the nation's iniquity had reached the brim. The first full cup was reached at Kadesh Barnea, when Israel's leaders rebelled. (See Numbers 14.) Oddly enough, the second full cup was reached when Israel violated 70 Sabbatical years.

When 70 Sabbath years had been violated, God summarily expelled Israel from Jerusalem and King Nebuchadnezzar hauled them off to Babylon. Israel had to remain in Babylon for 70 years because the land had missed 70 Sabbatical years of rest! Remember God's warning? **"All the time that it lies desolate, the land will have the rest it did not have** during the Sabbaths you lived in it." (Leviticus 26:35) In other words, God's patience with Israel reached its limit with 70 Sabbatical year violations and He evicted them from the land. Notice what the Bible says about their captivity: **"The land enjoyed its Sabbath rests; all the time of its desolation it rested, until the seventy years were completed in fulfillment of the word of the Lord spoken by Jeremiah."** (2 Chronicles 36:21)

Day/Year

Earlier I demonstrated how a day in the Jubilee calendar represents a literal year. Notice how God confirmed this to Israel through the prophet Ezekiel about 592 B.C.: **"Now, son of man, take a clay tablet, put it in front of you and draw the city of Jerusalem on it. Then lay siege to it: Erect siege works against it, build a ramp up to it, set up camps against it and put battering rams around it. Then take an iron pan, place it as an iron wall between you and the city and turn your face toward it. It will be under siege, and you shall besiege it. This will be a sign to the house of Israel. Then lie on your left side and put the sin of the house of Israel upon yourself. You are to bear their sin for the number of days you lie on your side. I have assigned you the same number of days as the years of their sin. So for 390 days you will bear the sin of the house of Israel. After you have finished this, lie down again, this time on your right side, and bear the sin of the house of Judah. I have assigned you 40 days, a day for each year."** (Ezekiel 4:1-6) The math involved in this passage confirms once again that a Jubilee cycle contains 49 – not 50 years. When the 390 years of Israel are added to the 40 offending years of Judah, there is a total of 430 years of sinful living. Notice, God did not reckon the sin of Judah and Israel as running concurrently. This is why Ezekiel had to first lay on his left side and then on his right side, indicating a total of 430 days – a day for each year. In 430 years, there are eight complete Jubilee cycles plus a partial cycle (the 9th) which contains 38 years. Incredible as it may seem, 430 years contain exactly 70 Sabbaticals! (Keep in mind that there are 8 Sabbaticals in a Jubilee cycle of 49 years.) Notice how the 70 Sabbaticals are calculated:

Eight Sabbaticals in Each Jubilee Cycle

Sabbatical Years in Jubilee Cycle

	Sun Year	Mon Year	Tue Year	Wed Year	Thu Year	Fri Year	Sab Year
First Jubilee Cycle							
Week 1	50/1 [1]	2	3	4	5	6	7 [2]
Week 2	8	9	10	11	12	13	14 [3]
Week 3	15	16	17	18	19	20	21 [4]
Week 4	22	23	24	25	26	27	28 [5]
Week 5	29	30	31	32	33	34	35 [6]
Week 6	36	37	38	39	40	41	42 [7]
Week 7	43	44	45	46	47	48	49 [8]

Small numbers indicate Sabbatical count.

Figure 6

430 Years Contain 70 Sabbaticals

Jubilee Cycle	Years in Cycle	No. of Sabbaticals
1	49	8
2	49	8
3	49	8
4	49	8
5	49	8
6	49	8
7	49	8
8	49	8
9	38	6
Total	430	70

Sabbatical Years in Last Jubilee Cycle

	Sun Year	Mon Year	Tue Year	Wed Year	Thu Year	Fri Year	Sab Year
	Ninth Jubilee Cycle						
Week 1	50/1 ^{1}	2	3	4	5	6	7 ^{2}
Week 2	8	9	10	11	12	13	14 ^{3}
Week 3	15	16	17	18	19	20	21 ^{4}
Week 4	22	23	24	25	26	27	28 ^{5}
Week 5	29	30	31	32	33	34	35 ^{6}
Week 6	36	37	38	39	40	41	42
Week 7	43	44	45	46	47	48	49

Small numbers indicate Sabbatical count.

Figure 7

To many people, these calculations may seem like a lot of numerical gibberish, but God was trying to teach Israel an important lesson. Notice what the Lord did when Israel paid for the 70 years of captivity in full (each year in captivity was exchanged for each Sabbath year violated): **"The land enjoyed its Sabbath rests; all the time of its desolation it rested, until the seventy years were completed in fulfillment of the word of the LORD spoken by Jeremiah. In the first year of Cyrus king of Persia, in order to fulfill the word of the Lord spoken by Jeremiah,** *the Lord moved* *the heart* of Cyrus king of Persia to make a proclamation throughout his realm and to put it in writing: 'This is what Cyrus king of Persia says: " 'The Lord, the God of heaven, has given me all the kingdoms of the Earth and he has appointed me to build a temple for him at Jerusalem in Judah. Anyone of his people among you – may the Lord his God be with him, and let him go up.' " (2 Chronicles 36:21-23; emphasis mine)

God is Timely

This next point fascinates me: God did not forget His people in Babylon. He moved the heart of King Cyrus to set His people free – right on time! This point is underscored again and again in the Old Testament. Notice the specifics: Israel left Egypt on the 15th day of the first month of their first calendar year. (Numbers 33:3) Then two years later, Israel stumbled at Kadesh Barnea when they sent the spies into the Promised Land. There, God's anger burned against them and He promised them 40 years of desert living! (Numbers 14:34) The adults, twenty years and older, of that first generation died in the wilderness. When the 40 years were completed, Israel's second generation entered the Promised Land on the 15th day of the first month during the 41st year – 40 years to the very day after leaving Egypt! (Joshua 5:10,11)

Another matter has to be considered. As far as God was concerned, the Jubilee calendar began two weeks *before* the Exodus. This conclusion is supported by two facts. First, when God punished the Israelites at Kadesh Barnea with 40 years in the wilderness, He did not count the 40 years from

Kadesh Barnea where the people rebelled; rather, He counted from the 15th day of the first month of the year of the Exodus. (Deuteronomy 2:14) Second, the Jubilee calendar must begin at the Exodus or the first or Sunday year of the 70th week (explained in more detail in the following paragraphs) is historically incorrect. These two factors combine to prove that God applied the day-for-a-year principle at Kadesh Barnea because the Jubilee calendar, which establishes the day/year principle, was in operation.

This small point is critical to correctly dating the Jubilee calendar. In other words, the termination of the calendar can only be as certain as the beginning point of the calendar.

Increasing Units of Time and Patience

While in Babylonian captivity, God spoke to the prophet Daniel and revealed that He was going to give Israel another chance. This opportunity, would have a limit of 70 units. (Remember, Israel went into captivity after violating 70 Sabbaticals.) However, instead of granting Israel 70 more Sabbaticals, God moved to the next larger unit within the calendar. He granted Israel 70 sevens (70 weeks of years – Daniel 9:24-27). With this offer, Israel would have no excuse for not becoming all God wanted. Note the incremental progression of units within the Jubilee calendar. First, God moved from 40 day/years in the wilderness to 70 Sabbatical-years in Babylon. Then, after 70 years in Babylon, God moved to 70 weeks of years for Israel. Notice the three increasing increments: Days – Sabbaticals – Weeks! God has a very important purpose in this progression. A careful analysis of God's timing reveals there are five progressions possible: 40 days – 70 Sabbaticals – 70 weeks – 70 Jubilee cycles – 70 centuries. (These last two time periods will be addressed momentarily. Remember the earlier assertion that sin would last 7,000 years? That assertion is partially based on the idea of increasing units of probationary time.)

One Week in the Jubilee Calendar Contains Seven Years

Toward the end of the Babylonian captivity (605-536 B.C.), God told Daniel that He was going to grant 70 weeks of Jubilee time to Israel for the purpose of putting away sin and bringing in everlasting righteousness. God also told Daniel that the 70 weeks would begin with the issuing of a decree to restore and rebuild Jerusalem. (Daniel 9:24-27) Reviewing history, we now know that four decrees were given for the restoration of Jerusalem. So, which decree did God have in mind? Answer: The third decree – given by Artaxerxes in 457 B.C. How can we be sure that God counted from the third decree? Easy! The proof is actually in the language of the prophecy because the prophecy uses Jubilee calendation! Bible students who have overlooked the importance of the Jubilee calendar have overlooked two significant points. First, God told Daniel that 70 'sevens' (70 weeks) were decreed for Israel: 70 weeks of 7 years = 70 x 7 = 490 solar years. Even though most scholars understand the 70 Jubilee weeks to represent 490 literal years, they do not consider the fact that 70 weeks happens to be exactly 10 Jubilee cycles (49 X 10 = 490). The significance of this cannot be overstated. This tiny point completely eliminates the possibility that the

70th week mentioned in Daniel 9 can occur at some time in the future. According to the Jubilee calendar, the 70th week can only occur sequentially after the 69th week. Jubilee weeks cannot be separated from each other any more than weeks can be separated in our calendar today. Week 69 follows week 68 and week 70 follows week 69! Second, the prophecy indicates that Messiah would appear "after 7 weeks and 62 weeks" had expired (a total of 69 weeks). Most scholars overlook the fact that God expressly said 7 weeks and 62 weeks. They conclude that the total actually points to 69 weeks without realizing that God actually said the following (paraphrasing): "The 70 weeks begin with the decree to rebuild Jerusalem. The decree that matters is the one that is synchronous with a Jubilee cycle (7 weeks). Then, 62 weeks after that Jubilee cycle passes, the 70th week will begin. In the middle of the 70th week, Messiah will be "cut off" and confirm the covenant of salvation." (Daniel 9:24-27) The events occurred right on time, just as God predicted! In fact, the understanding of this prophecy convinced the wise men from the East that Messiah's birth had taken place. (Matthew 2:2)

Briefly, here are the historical facts surrounding the prophecy of 70 weeks. On or about the first day of the first month in the Jubilee year of 457 B.C., King Artaxerxes issued a decree granting permission to restore Jerusalem and the temple. Ezra began his preparations to return to Jerusalem on the first day of the first month (Spring) of the year 457 B.C. (Ezra 7:9) He finally left Babylon with the decree in hand on the 12th day of the first month (Ezra 8:31) and arrived in Jerusalem on the first day of the fifth month (our July/August) (Ezra 7:9).

Right on Time

The timing of the king's decree, issued during the first few days of the first month of 457 B.C., was not coincidental. God moved Artaxerxes' heart to write the restoration decree just as the Jubilee year began. After all, the decree was in keeping with Jubilee restoration! God saw to it that the land was given back to its original owners! The king issued the decree *right on time*. The Bible also records how God moved the heart of King Cyrus to write the release from Babylon *right on time*. (2 Chronicles 36:22) This should not surprise anyone. God's timing is always purposeful and accurate.

Jubilee Cycle After Artaxerxes' Decree

Jubilee Cycle Number 21 – 457 B.C. to 409 B.C.						
	Sun	Mon	Tue	Wed	Thu	Fri	Sab
Week 1	457	456	455	454	453	452	451
Week 2	450	449	448	447	446	445	444
Week 3	443	442	441	440	439	438	437
Week 4	436	435	434	433	432	431	430
Week 5	429	428	427	426	425	424	423
Week 6	422	421	420	419	418	417	416
Week 7	415	414	413	412	411	410	409

Figure 8

Jubilee Cycles Between 457 B.C. and A.D. 33

Cycle Number	Jubilee Yr.	Sabbatical Year						
21	457 B.C.	451	444	437	430	423	416	409
22	408 B.C.	402	395	388	381	374	367	360
23	359 B.C.	353	346	339	332	325	318	311
24	310 B.C.	304	297	290	283	276	269	262
25	261 B.C.	255	248	241	234	227	220	213
26	212 B.C.	206	199	192	185	178	171	164
27	163 B.C.	157	150	143	136	129	122	115
28	114 B.C.	108	101	94	87	80	73	66
29	65 B.C.	59	52	45	38	31	24	17
30	16 B.C.	10	3	5 A.D.	12	19	26	33

Figure 9

Since God's calendar operates from Spring equinox to Spring equinox, the 69 weeks predicted in Daniel 9 span a period of time from the Spring of 457 B.C. to the Spring of A.D. 27. The 70th and final week of seven years began in the Spring of A.D. 27. During that year Jesus was baptized and began His ministry. (A.D. 27 is the Sunday year or first year of the 70th week, A.D. 28 was the Monday year, etc.) Luke 3 pinpoints the historical location writing, **"In the fifteenth year of the reign of Tiberius Caesar – when Pontius Pilate was governor of Judea, Herod tetrarch of Galilee, his brother Philip tetrarch of Iturea and Traconitis, and Lysanias tetrarch of Abilene – {2} during the high priesthood of Annas and Caiaphas, the word of God came to**

John son of Zechariah in the desert ... {21} When all the people were being baptized, Jesus was baptized too ... {23} Now Jesus himself was about thirty years old when he began his ministry. He was the son, so it was thought, of Joseph, the son of Heli." (Luke 3:1-2,21,23)

Note: Some Bible students claim that the Jubilee calendar operates from Fall-to-Fall. This is not true. It is true that the Jews observed a Fall-to-Fall civil calendar after the Babylonian captivity, but the Jubilee calendar, God's calendar, dates from the Exodus, which occurred 800 years *before* the Babylonian captivity. The prophecy of Daniel 9 also indicates that Messiah would be "cut off" in the middle of the 70th week. Ever accurate, God's calendar, using the weekly cycle of years, pinpoints the year of Christ's death as A.D. 30. Remember, a Jubilee year begins in the Spring. So, the Sunday year began in the Spring of A.D. 27 and the Wednesday year is the middle year of the week. Jesus died on the 14th day of the first month in A.D. 30, at the time of Passover.

The 70th Week Jubilee Cycle 30 (See Figure 9 on Previous Page)							
	Sun	Mon	Tue	Wed	Thu	Fri	Sab
Calendar Year (A.D.)	27	28	29	30	31	32	33

Figure 10

While the historical and prophetic harmony of these matters is impressive and very interesting to investigate, there is a matter of greater importance occurring that needs to be recognized. *The ministry and death of Jesus confirms the synchronism of the whole Jubilee calendar.* In other words, by associating a known year with a day of the week, we can easily determine the day of the week for any year – past, present or future. Surely then, the words of Paul make a lot of sense: **"But when the time had fully come, God sent his Son, born of a woman, born under law."** (Galatians 4:4)

Try to understand this point. The weekly cycle of years is an unbroken chain, just like the weekly cycle of days is an unbroken chain. When Jesus came to Earth, He confirmed which year was the Sunday year or first year of the weekly cycle (A.D. 27) and which year was the Wednesday year, the middle year of the weekly cycle (A.D. 30) by his baptism and death. Once we know the synchronism of the years (which day of the week corresponds to a particular year), we discover a number of other things about timing that would be otherwise unknown.

For example, the Biblical and historical evidence confirms that the decree of Artaxerxes was issued in a Jubilee year (Sunday year). Further, the Jubilee year of 457 B.C. correctly synchronizes with Hezekiah's 15th year – the only Jubilee year mentioned in the Bible! Using the unbroken chain of the week of years, we can also pinpoint the seventh-year under discussion in Jeremiah 34:12-21 as 591 B.C. because this would be the only Sabbatical year within Zedekiah's reign of 11 years. This is the beauty of knowing the synchronism of the week of years – we are able to date events that otherwise could not be known for sure. Once the operation of God's Jubilee calendar is understood, the chronology of events becomes much clearer and more forceful.

A sad footnote: When the 70 weeks had expired (A.D. 33), the Jews still failed to cooperate with God. The Jews had willfully rebelled against God's own Son; so, in A.D. 70, He sent the Romans to Jerusalem and destroyed the city. (Luke 21:23; Matthew 23:38)

7 x 10 = 70 = The End?

Perhaps you have noticed how biblical limits seem to be measured in units of 70. For example, there were seventy elders in Israel. (Exodus 24:9) The silver bowls used by temple priests weighed 70 shekels. (Numbers 7:13) The number of Jacob's family that went down into Egypt was 70. (Deuteronomy 10:22) God killed 70 men for looking into the Ark of the Covenant. (1 Samuel 6:19) Israel was in Babylon for 70 years. (2 Chronicles 36:21) It seems more than coincidental that the length of man's life is often called threescore and ten, which is 70. (Psalms 90:10, Isaiah 23:15)

You may have already considered the possibility that the total existence for sin could be 7,000 years, which just happens to be 70 centuries. The point here is that 70 units often represent a limit. Notice also how 70 is reached. The number seven often represents a complete or full number (seven trumpets, seven seals, seven bowls, etc.), and when the number 10 magnifies the number seven, the result appears to reflect a divine limit. For example, the Day of Atonement occurred as a function of 7 and 10 (7th month – 10th day). The dragon in Revelation 12 and the dragon-like beast in chapter 13 have 7 heads and 10 horns.

Consider this: The total number of Jubilee cycles granted to Israel was 30 from the Exodus to the end of the 70th week – the last 10 cycles were the 70 weeks of Daniel 9. (See Figure 9, page 170.) If the Jubilee calendar terminated in 1994 with 70 cycles, the apparent number of Jubilee cycles for the Gentiles (the times of the Gentiles mentioned in Luke 21:24) would be 40 (A.D. 34 – 1994). Does the calendar terminate in 1994? I believe so. Not just because the numerical count seems complete, but because future prophetic time-periods also agree harmoniously with the 7,000 year template of the weekly cycle if the day/year principle is brought to an end.

Prophetic Time Periods

It is beyond the scope of this appendix to examine all the corporate prophetic time periods in the Bible. However, a point about the fourth apocalyptic rule given on page 23 must be made: *All apocalyptic time periods occurring during the presence of Jubilee cycles are to be interpreted in Jubilee units of time. Under the Jubilee calendar, a day represents a literal solar year.* (An apocalyptic time period is a time period that occurs in one of the 18 apocalyptic prophecies of Daniel and Revelation. For example, the "seven times" that were to pass over king Nebuchadnezzar are to be reckoned as seven literal years since the prophecy in Daniel 4:24,32 is not one of the apocalyptic prophecies.) This rule also means that apocalyptic time periods that occur outside the operation of Jubilee calendar are to be interpreted as literal units of time. This concept becomes very interesting when we consider the possibility that there could be a finite number of Jubilee cycles. That number could be 70.

Here is how the Jubilee principle works with respect to prophetic time periods. Before Jubilee cycles were given, prophetic time-periods were literal. Therefore, Noah's 120 years of warning (Genesis 6:3) are reckoned as 120 literal years because they happened *before* the Jubilee cycles began. The 40 years of wandering in the wilderness was measured in day/year units because the Jubilee calendar began at the time of the Exodus, not with Israel's entrance into the Promised Land. (See Deuteronomy 2:14, Numbers 14:34.) The 1,260 days of Daniel 7:25, and Revelation 12:6,14 are considered a day for a year because they occurred *before* 70 Jubilee cycles ended in 1994. Therefore, they represent a 1,260 year time-period. The 1,000 years of the seventh millennium will be literal years because they occur *after* the 70th Jubilee cycle expired in the Spring of 1994.

The expiration of the Jubilee calendar resolves several problems regarding time periods in Daniel and Revelation. For example: The 1,335 days found in Daniel 12 are literal, the 42 months in Revelation 13:5 are literal and the five months of torture during the fifth trumpet are also literal. (Revelation 9:5) Since each of these time periods occur *after* the Jubilee cycles end, they are literal days instead of prophetic years.

Jubilee Cycles After A.D. 70

Two prophecies continue to confirm the perpetuity of Jubilee cycles long after the death of Christ or the demise of ancient Israel in A.D 70. The first prophecy is found in Daniel 7:25. In this prophecy, the Bible says the little horn power would persecute the saints of God for a time, times and half of time. This time period covers the period of the "Dark Ages" that lasted 1,260 day/years. It began in A.D. 538 and ended in 1798 when the Pope was imprisoned. History confirms that this time period has been fulfilled. Even more, it verifies that the day/year principle existed and operated long after the death of Christ in A.D. 30 or the destruction of Jerusalem in A.D. 70. The fulfillment of Daniel 7:25 confirms the operating presence of the Jubilee calendar, for without it, there is no consistent principle which demands that the day/year mechanism be used.

The second prophecy confirming the perpetuity of the Jubilee cycle long after ancient Israel's demise is located in Daniel 8:14. Since this prophecy began 457 years before Christ and extends until A.D. 1844, three points must be emphasized. First, the day/year principle is at work. Since the first ten Jubilee cycles (70 sevens or 490 literal years) granted to Israel are considered day/year as a result of the Jubilee calendar, and the 70 weeks are "cut off" from the longer prophecy of 2,300 days, then the 2,300 day prophecy must be calculated in day/year units just like the 70 weeks, for they run concurrently. Second, the 2,300 day prophecy demonstrates that Christ's ministry in the Heavenly sanctuary is intimately connected to the operation of Jubilee cycles. One last point on this topic. If the Jubilee calendar came to an end at Christ's death as many scholars claim, then the 70th week was never finished. Instead of covering 70 weeks, as the prophecy predicted, it would have only covered 69½ weeks! (For further study on the day/year principle and the operation of the Jubilee calendar, my book *The Revelation of Jesus*, provides a deeper examination of these matters. See the list of study helps at the back of this book.)

How 1437 B.C. is Calculated

The date of the Exodus is very important to this study since the ending date of 70 Jubilee cycles can only be established if the beginning date is also identified. In other words, according to my calculations, the Spring of 1994 marks the end of 70 Jubilee cycles because the first Jubilee cycle began in 1437 B.C.! It is not a complicated procedure to calculate 1437 B.C. as the date of the Exodus, but it is somewhat tedious. Here are the five steps necessary to validate the date of the Exodus:

Step 1. God carefully designated the beginning point of His calendar two weeks before the Exodus by identifying the 1st day - 1st month - 1st year. God's year operates from Spring (equinox) to Spring (equinox). (See Exodus 12:1-12; 40:17.) (Note: When I write about a Jubilee year such as A.D. 33, I am referring to a time period that reaches from March A.D. 33 to March A.D. 34. For simplicity, I call it A.D. 33 because the Jubilee year began in the Spring of Julian A.D. 33

and the bulk of the Jubilee year occurs during that Julian year.)

Step 2. Jesus began His ministry on time (A.D. 27 – a Sunday year) and He died on time – in the middle of the 70th week (A.D. 30 – a Wednesday year) – counting weeks from the decree of Artaxerxes. (See Luke 3:21-23 and Daniel 9:27.) If weeks of years are counted from their origin at the Exodus, then Jesus died in the middle of the 210th week which also happens to be the last week in 30 Jubilee cycles. Counting weeks of years from Artaxerxes' decree, makes Jesus' death occur in the middle of the 70th week (just as the prophecy indicates).

The 70th and 71st Week							
	Sun	Mon	Tue	Wed	Thu	Fri	Sab
Week 70 (A.D.)	27	28	29	30	31	32	33
Week 71 (A.D.)	34	35	36	37	38	39	40

Figure 11

Step 3. If A.D. 30 = Wednesday year, then the following is true:

457 B.C. = Sunday year (Figure 9, page 170)

1437 B.C. = Sunday year (457 B.C. plus twenty 49 year cycles)

1388 B.C. = Sunday year (1437 B.C. minus one 49 year cycle)

A.D. 1994 = Sunday year (Keep on reading.)

The 70 weeks prophecy began in the Spring of the Sunday year (457 B.C.) with the decree of Artaxerxes and ended with the 70th Sabbatical year A.D. 33. A total of 490 years (counting from Spring to Spring) elapsed. The decree by Artaxerxes was issued in the first days of Spring, 457 B.C. (See Ezra 6:19; 7:9 and 8:31.).

Step 4. The Bible identifies the date of a Jubilee year during the 15th year of King Hezekiah. **"In the fourteenth year of King Hezekiah's reign, Sennacherib king of Assyria attacked all the fortified cities of Judah and captured them."** [Isaiah said to the king] **"This will be the sign for you, O Hezekiah: 'This year** [your fourteenth] **you will eat what grows by itself, and the second year** [your 15th year] **what springs from that. But in the third year sow and reap, plant vineyards and eat their fruit.' "** (See Isaiah 36:1, 37:30.)

This Jubilee year can be accurately identified because King Sennacherib had to be in power and Jubilee years are always Sunday years. A historical review reveals that Sennacherib was in power about 705 B.C. So, the 15th year of Hezekiah has to occur *after* 705 B.C. and the first Sunday year after 705 B.C. is 702 B.C. We can determine if the first Sunday year is the Jubilee year within Sennacherib's reign by starting with the well known date of 586 B.C., when Jerusalem was finally destroyed by Nebuchadnezzar, and then count backwards through the reign of kings to Hezekiah's 15th year. (See next page.)

Time Between Hezekiah and Jerusalem's Destruction			
King	Regnal*	Actual	Date (B.C.)
Hezekiah**	14	11	702
Manesseh	55	54	692
Amon	2	2	638
Josiah	31	29	636
Jehoiakim	11	10	607
Jehoiachin	0.25	0.25	597
Zedekiah	11	11	596
Jerusalem's Third			586
Total Years	125*	118	

Figure 12

* A regnal year is counted as a year on the throne – even if it is only a partial year. A regnal year is also credited to a king even if two kings reign at the same time. For example, David and Solomon (Father - Son) were kings of Israel at the same time. They both reigned 40 regnal years, but the actual number of years they reigned over Israel does not equal 80 years. The custom in ancient times was for the two kings to reign concurrently for a few years to stabilize the authority of the incoming king, especially if he was a young heir to the throne.

** During Hezekiah's 14th year, God gave him a promise of 15 more years of life – so his total reign would last about

29 years. (Isaiah 38:5) The Jubilee year occurred during his 15th year on the throne – leaving him about 14 more years of life. I assume that Hezekiah placed his heir, Manesseh, on the throne when he turned 12 years old. In this manner, before Hezekiah died, he could teach Manesseh the ways of the court. (After all, Hezekiah knew the year he was going to die.) Thus, Hezekiah reigned for a total of 29 years, but he reigned alone for about 26 years.

Note: Regnal years for this time-period total 125 years, but the actual years are 118. The seven years of overlapping is well within the number of years allowed by scholars for this time-period. Many scholars allow 10 years of co-regent reign for this list of kings.

Summarizing: From Jesus' death in the middle year of the 70th week (A.D. 30 – the Wednesday year), we can determine the date of all Sunday years. Hezekiah's 15th year is a Sunday/Jubilee year combination which follows a 49th Sabbatical year. We also know that Hezekiah's 15th year has to occur after Sennacherib came to power in 705 B.C. One date, 702 B.C., exclusively satisfies the parameters. Other Sunday years are either too early or too late to meet all of the specifications. Notice the impact of this conclusion: If 702 B.C. is correctly identified as a Jubilee year, then Artaxerxes' decree in 457 B.C. was a Jubilee year as well because it falls on the exact multiple of 49 year cycles with 702 B.C.! When one Jubilee year is known, then all Jubilee years can be calculated – forward or backward. For example, A.D. 34 is a Sunday year, and it is also a Jubilee year.

So, we can conclude that the year of the Exodus is year 1 of the Jubilee calendar. It is a Sunday year because Sunday is the first day/year in the calendar. The Sunday year of the Exodus must synchronize with 702 B.C., 457 B.C., the 70 weeks, and of course, the 70th week. Good news, it does!

Step 5. The last step is to identify the timing of Solomon's reign because we can leapfrog from the year of the Exodus to the fourth year of Solomon. **"In the four hundred and eightieth year after the Israelites had come out of Egypt, in the fourth year of Solomon's reign over Israel, in the month of Ziv, the second month, he began to build the temple of the Lord."** (1 Kings 6:1) The approximate dating of Solomon's reign is another marker which helps us to determine the exact year of the Exodus because it has to be a Jubilee year. We know that 702 B.C., 457 B.C. and the dates of the 70th week are perfectly synchronized. So, by checking the 49 year cycles within the era of the Exodus *and* Solomon's reign, one of the following dates has to be the year of the Exodus:

1486 B.C.   **1437 B.C.**   1388 B.C.   1339 B.C.

Providentially, there is well confirmed, widely accepted data outside the Bible showing that Ahab, king of Israel was killed during the 22nd year of his reign in 852 B.C. We also know that the time period between Solomon's 4th year and Ahab's death is a period of 120 regnal years (it turns out to be 106 actual years). Here are the regnal years (as recorded in the Bible) from Solomon's 4th year to the 22nd year of Ahab's reign:

Regnal Years From Solomon to Ahab	
King	Regnal Years
Solomon	36
Jeroboam	22
Nadab	2
Baasha	24
Elah	2
Zimri	1 Week
Omri	12
Ahab	22
Total Regnal Years	120

Figure 13

If we calculate the date of the Exodus using these regnal years, we find:

The date of Ahab's death:	852 B.C.
Plus regnal years back to Solomon:	120
Plus 480 back to Exodus:	480

Possible Date of the Exodus: **1452 B.C.**

But, 1452 B.C. is not a Jubilee year nor is 1452 a Sunday year. Moving forward in time to the closest Jubilee year (regnal years always total more than actual years), we find:

The date of Ahab's death: 852 B.C.
Add 106 actual years: 106 (reducing regnal years by 14)
Add 480 back to Exodus: 480

Date of the Exodus: 1437 B.C.

The difference between regnal and actual years for Solomon and Ahab is 14. This is well within the tolerance allowed for the succession of eight kings. Some scholars reduce the regnal years for this time period by five and say the actual years are 115 instead of 106. But, the records of co-regent reigns during this time-period are nonexistent. So, the actual years must remain within the realm of educated guessing. However, the Jubilee calendar imposes a "timing matrix" on this time period. Here is why: The Exodus has to occur during a Jubilee year (Sunday year). Second, the span of time between the Exodus and Solomon/Ahab has to begin with Jubilee calendar year one and conclude in 852 B.C. Finally, the Bible limits the span of time between Solomon and Ahab to 120 regnal years. So, 1437 B.C. is the only year that can qualify for the Exodus. It is a Sunday year and it is the first year of the Jubilee calendar. In addition, 1437 B.C. occurs within the time-frame allotted by Scripture. All other Jubilee years under consideration are too near or far away from the regnal or actual reigns of the kings to qualify. Therefore, 1437 B.C. becomes the *exclusive date* of the Exodus and the expiration of 70 complete Jubilee cycles (3,430 years) occurred at the Spring equinox on March 20, 1994.

Incidently, 70 Jubilee cycles equals 490 weeks of years – just like 70 weeks equals 490 years. If the Jubilee calendar expired in March 1994, with 70 Jubilee cycles completed, we can assume that future prophetic time periods are to be reckoned in literal units. In fact, if the prophetic time-periods of Daniel and Revelation are deemed to be literal, the year 2000 is the earliest possible date for the 6,000th year. Keep in mind that there is a margin of error of about 20 years. The 6,000th year is coming and we are moving toward it – one day at a time. The real value of the Jubilee calendar is not so much the placement of historical events, as helpful as this is. Rather, the beauty of the Jubilee calendar today provides a simple, but profound explanation of why God reckons some prophecies as a day-for-a-year and others as literal time. This little key opens up a new world of discovery about the literal timing of end-time events.

Revelation's Time-Periods and 1994

There is a prophetic mechanism that says: Prophetic things are only understood on or about the time of fulfillment. The understanding of Revelation is now open for study and investigation because the events it describes are about to be fulfilled. God has kept these things hidden until now so that our discovery of His truth would motivate us to prepare for His appearing.

I began this Appendix by saying there are many time periods mentioned in Daniel and Revelation. For example, there will be 42 months of persecution by Babylon. (Revelation 13:5) The Two Witnesses will empower the 144,000 for

The First 35 Jubilee Cycles of 49 Years Each

Event	Jubilee Cycle #	Jubilee	1	2	3	4	5	6	7
			Years						
			Sabbatical Dates for Each Cycle						
Exodus	1	1437	1431	1424	1417	1410	1403	1396	1389
	2	1388	1382	1375	1368	1361	1354	1347	1340
	3	1339	1333	1326	1319	1312	1305	1298	1291
	4	1290	1284	1277	1270	1263	1256	1249	1242
	5	1241	1235	1228	1221	1214	1207	1200	1193
	6	1192	1186	1179	1172	1165	1158	1151	1144
	7	1143	1137	1130	1123	1116	1109	1102	1095
	8	1094	1088	1081	1074	1067	1060	1053	1046
	9	1045	1039	1032	1025	1018	1011	1004	997
	10	996	990	983	976	969	962	955	948
	11	947	941	934	927	920	913	906	899
Ahab Dies in 852 B.C.	12	898	892	885	878	871	864	857	850
	13	849	843	836	829	822	815	808	801
	14	800	794	787	780	773	766	759	752
	15	751	745	738	731	724	717	710	703
Jubilee in Bible	16	702	696	689	682	675	668	661	654
	17	653	647	640	633	626	619	612	605
	18	604	598	591	584	577	570	563	556
	19	555	549	542	535	528	521	514	507
	20	506	500	493	486	479	472	465	458
Decree to Rebuild	21	457	451	444	437	430	423	416	409
	22	408	402	395	388	381	374	367	360
	23	359	353	346	339	332	325	318	311
	24	310	304	297	290	283	276	269	262
	25	261	255	248	241	234	227	220	213
	26	212	206	199	192	185	178	171	164
	27	163	157	150	143	136	129	122	115
	28	114	108	101	94	87	80	73	66
	29	65	59	52	45	38	31	24	17
70ᵗʰ Week	30	16	10	3 B.C.	A.D. 5	12	19	26	33
Christian Era Begins A.D. 34	31	34	40	47	54	61	68	75	82
	32	83	89	96	103	110	117	124	131
	33	132	138	145	152	159	166	173	180
	34	181	187	194	201	208	215	222	229
	35	230	236	243	250	257	264	271	278

Highlighted range is the 70 weeks prophecy of Daniel 9. *Figure 14*

The Second 35 Jubilee Cycles of 49 Years Each

Event	Jubilee Cycle #	Jubilee	Years						
			Sabbatical Dates for Each Cycle						
			1	2	3	4	5	6	7
	36	279	285	292	299	306	313	320	327
	37	328	334	341	348	355	362	369	376
	38	377	383	390	397	404	411	418	425
	39	426	432	439	446	453	460	467	474
	40	475	481	488	495	502	509	516	523
	41	524	530	537	544	551	558	565	572
	42	573	579	586	593	600	607	614	621
	43	622	628	635	642	649	656	663	670
	44	671	677	684	691	698	705	712	719
	45	720	726	733	740	747	754	761	768
	46	769	775	782	789	796	803	810	817
	47	818	824	831	838	845	852	859	866
	48	867	873	880	887	894	901	908	915
	49	916	922	929	936	943	950	957	964
	50	965	971	978	985	992	999	1006	1013
	51	1014	1020	1027	1034	1041	1048	1055	1062
	52	1063	1069	1076	1083	1090	1097	1104	1111
	53	1112	1118	1125	1132	1139	1146	1153	1160
	54	1161	1167	1174	1181	1188	1195	1202	1209
	55	1210	1216	1223	1230	1237	1244	1251	1258
	56	1259	1265	1272	1279	1286	1293	1300	1307
	57	1308	1314	1321	1328	1335	1342	1349	1356
	58	1357	1363	1370	1377	1384	1391	1398	1405
	59	1406	1412	1419	1426	1433	1440	1447	1454
	60	1455	1461	1468	1475	1482	1489	1496	1503
	61	1504	1510	1517	1524	1531	1538	1545	1552
	62	1553	1559	1566	1573	1580	1587	1594	1601
	63	1602	1607	1615	1622	1629	1636	1643	1650
	64	1651	1657	1664	1671	1678	1685	1692	1699
	65	1700	1706	1713	1720	1727	1734	1741	1748
	66	1749	1755	1762	1769	1776	1783	1790	1797
Protestant Era Begins 1798	67	1798	1804	1811	1818	1825	1832	1839	1846
	68	1847	1853	1860	1867	1874	1881	1888	1895
	69	1896	1902	1909	1916	1923	1930	1937	1944
	70	1945	1951	1958	1965	1972	1979	1986	1993

The 70th Jubilee Cycle Ended on March 20, 1994 (Spring Equinox)   *Figure 15*

1,260 days. (Revelation 11:3) The torment of the fifth trumpet will last five literal months. (Revelation 9:5) The millennium is 1,000 literal years in length. (Revelation 20) The point is that these time periods carefully harmonize with the operation of the Jubilee calendar. These time periods are literal units of time because the Jubilee calendar, with its day/year mechanism, has expired.

God is giving good clues about Revelation's meaning. Less than three months after the Jubilee calendar was completed, He underscored the significance of His calendar. From July 16 to 22, 1994, the largest interplanetary impact in our solar system during recorded history occurred when comet Shoemaker-Levy 9 slammed into Jupiter. Scientists are now predicting the same catastrophes that were predicted in Revelation 2,000 years ago. In fact, they are doing a better job of heralding these events than most ministers who are unwilling to investigate the book of Revelation. The watchmen have fallen asleep at their posts and have failed to warn the world of God's coming wrath! World conditions are ripe for a catastrophic conclusion. There is much talk of peace and safety, but the hearts of many have waxed cold. There is no love, peace, or safety outside of Jesus. As in Noah's day, the world is beyond restoration. Politicians can only offer an illusion of solving the complex problems the world faces.

Present Truth

Truth is like a bulb that lies hidden in the soil. At the proper time each Spring, the bulb begins to grow. Once the flower of present truth opens, its beauty cannot be silenced. Hope and encouragement radiate from beauty. In a similar way, a number of Bible themes have come together to help us understand that we are living in the last days. It has not been possible in this brief appendix to prove every point. In fact, I may not be able to prove many points to your satisfaction. In the final analysis though, I have tried to bring hope. The coming of Jesus is imminent. The Holy Spirit bears witness to this fact. So, let's get ready to go home by seeking purity of heart and character. Let's do everything we can to invite our loved ones and friends, and even those we do not know, to come along.

Summary

The historical fulfillment of several prophetic time-periods suggests that the Jubilee calendar year is an important principle behind prophetic reckoning. For this reason, 1994 appears to be a significant year because 1994 appears to be a line of demarcation – separating day/year time-periods from literal time-periods. We see that the crown-jewel of the weekly cycle, the seventh-day Sabbath, serves as a template of the coming "Sabbatical Millennium." The seventh millennium has to begin on time. God's purposes know no haste nor delay. Those who live during the Great Tribulation will see just how important God's holy day is to our Creator. Just as the Sabbath-year was a test of faith to Israel of old (Exodus 16:4), the Sabbath day, the seventh day of the week, will be a 'Sabbath-rest test' to the remnant of Israel. The weekly cycle serves as a template of the Jubilee cycle. We learned that God's patience with Israel was reached with 70 violations of Sabbatical years, then He removed them as trustees of the gospel. The Jubilee cycles point out that God's patience with man has a limit. Soon, the 144,000 will receive great Holy Spirit power. They will present the truth about God that will be so present and essential for our time. Billions will hear their message and millions will be saved as a result.

God has set a limit for the duration of sin. God will have a people on Earth who understand what He is about to do *before* He does it. This is why Revelation's story is important. Ordinary people, empowered by the Holy Spirit, will testify during that awful day what God wants. God will have a people who have done their homework and put their prophetic faith in order. God will have a prepared people who are ready and willing to go, to be and to do all that He asks. This group of people will go forward in the Spirit and power of Elijah during the Great Tribulation and they will be especially blessed for their faith. Now that 1994 has passed, we have crossed over the line of demarcation. All future prophetic time-periods will be reckoned in literal time. All that remains now is for prophesied events to begin.

Supplemental Bible Study Helps

Bible Study Helps - Audio and Video Tapes

The following is a sample listing of seminar studies on Bible prophecy. Tapes may be purchased individually or as a set from a seminar series, such as seen on TV. Keep in mind that each tape is a building block, therefore, no one presentation is complete within itself.

Daniel's Prophetic Visions – A series outlining the prophetic significance of Daniel's visions which form a foundation for understanding the book of Revelation. (Set includes 6 video tapes for 12 audio tapes.)

Studies on the Book of Revelation – Sample topics in this series include: The seven seals, the seven trumpets, the beasts in Revelation, the 144,000, the two witnesses and the mark of the beast, etc. (Set includes 12 video tapes or 24 audio tapes.)

Studies on the Plan of Salvation – Sample topics in this series include: Who is Jesus, the origin of sin, mercy and justice, righteousness-by-faith, the sanctuary services, the Jubilee calendar and the Sabbath-rest test. (Set includes 5 video tapes or 10 audio tapes.)

Additional Bible Study Helps - Books and Charts

1. *The Revelation of Jesus* This book (346 pages) serves as the primary textbook for seminar study. This book not only addresses coming events, it presents a historical setting for understanding how the prophecies operate. It also contains several diagrams and charts on Daniel and Revelation.

2. *Day Star* Newsletter A monthly newsletter that contains Bible studies on topics relating to current issues and/or the prophetic stories found in Daniel and Revelation. Some remaining back issues are available.

3. *18 End-Time Bible Prophecies* This book is a verse-by-verse commentary on the 18 apocalyptic prophecies found in Daniel and Revelation. It is written in a parallel format with the *New International Version* Bible. (282 pages)

4. *5 Essential Bible Truths* – Pamphlets explaining five fundamental truths that help lay a foundation necessary for understanding the end-time story.

5. **Mysteries of Daniel Vol. I and Mysteries of Revelation Vol. II** - Small, pocket size books with a verse-by-verse commentary on Daniel and Revelation.

6. **Charts and other study helps**

Wake Up America Seminars, Inc.
P.O. Box 273, Bellbrook, Ohio 45305
(513) 848-3322

– Proclaiming Revelation's Story –